The Adult Piano Method
Play By Choice

With The Music YOU Want To Play! By Fred Kern

Editor: Barbara Kreader

HAL•LEONARD
CORPORATION

7777 W. BLUEMOUND RD. P.O. BOX 13819 MILWAUKEE, WI 53213

B I O G R A P H Y

Fred Kern is Professor of Music and a Specialist in Piano Education at the University of North Texas where he has been Director of Piano Pedagogy and Group Piano Studies since 1980. In addition to being an independent piano teacher, Kern has taught band, chorus, and general music in public schools, and he was formerly on the piano faculties of Harper College and Northwestern University. He holds a BS degree in music education from Illinois State, a MM in piano performance from Illinois Wesleyan, a MM in piano pedagogy from Northwestern University and a Doctor of Arts in piano performance and pedagogy from the University of Northern Colorado.

In 1985, Kern was selected to teach in the first Summer Music Institute at Tunghai University in the Republic of China. He has served as a leader and active member of the National Conference on Piano Pedagogy, the Music Teachers National Association, and the Texas Music Educators Association, in addition to being a member of the Honorary Advisory Board of the Roland ISM Alliance and the advisory board of the National Piano Teachers Institute. He holds the Master Teacher Certificate given by MTNA and is well-known as a clinician, author, composer, and arranger of texts and piano teaching materials.

I N T R O D U C T I O N

As an adult, you are studying piano by your own choice. As an already independent individual, you have specific personal reasons for wanting to play the piano, maybe even some long-neglected dream and desire to be a pianist. In addition, you probably exhibit well-defined musical tastes, and your motivation to study springs from your desire to play music you like.

PLAY BY CHOICE ADULT PIANO METHOD was designed for adult beginners like you with **your** primary goal in mind: being able to play rewarding music after putting forth a reasonable effort. You are accustomed to making choices in all aspects of your life, and you want your music study to give you the same opportunity to choose. PLAY BY CHOICE ADULT PIANO METHOD has been written in a way that allows you to reach the goals you set for yourself. From the very beginning and at each level of progress, you have some choice in the pieces you practice and so you will be studying music you like.

You will find all the music conveniently located in one place: The PIECES BY CHOICE pull-out section. It includes the familiar classic, pop, ragtime, religious, movie themes, and folk tunes every adult wants to play. These pieces appear in sets and coordinate with each chapter of the PLAY BY CHOICE course book.

Each chapter features one or more required (PIECES NO CHOICE) for emphasis and instruction.

You will also discover several (PIECES BY CHOICE) . You may select and perfect one or more of these pieces according to your interests and tastes.

The course then allows you to consult the four sections of the chapter that will teach you how to play each piece. Every chapter presents the following divisions that answer your questions:

What's new?	**FACTS** (The musical concepts)
Where do I start?	**PREPS** (Preparation for playing)
How should I practice?	**REPS** (Efficient practice suggestions)
What else can I do?	**CHALLENGES** (Extended learning possibilities)

If you wish you play other pieces in different styles at each chapter level, look for the MORE FOR YOUR ADULT METHOD supplementary library at your local music store. The chart at the front of each book will help you determine which pieces fit with the levels in each chapter.

Best of all, every choice makes music, especially when played with the accompaniments and backgrounds available for separate purchase on disk, CD, or tape.

BEST WISHES as you begin PLAY BY CHOICE ADULT PIANO METHOD.

Fred Kern

CHAPTER : Piano Basics & Black Keys

Pieces No Choice

Each chapter features one or more required pieces for emphasis and instruction.

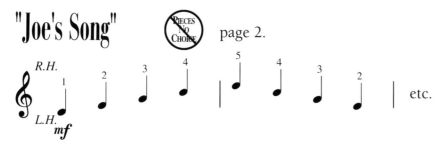

"Joe's Song"   (PIECES NO CHOICE)   page 2.

Pieces By Choice

In all chapters, you may choose to select and perfect one or more of the PIECES BY CHOICE. Learn them as solos, but also play them as duets when the Disk/CD/Tape or your teacher plays the accompaniment.

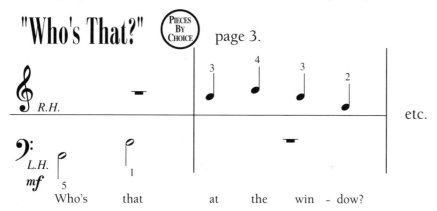

"Who's That?"   (PIECES BY CHOICE)   page 3.

Who's that at the win - dow?

6 Facts

(Beat, Measures and Barlines, Notes and Rests (♩ 𝅗𝅥 o 𝄿 ▬ ▬), Repeat (:||), Hand Position, Fingering, Keyboard Direction, Dynamics (*f*, *p*, *mf*))

1 Preps

(Tap and Count, Lap Taps, Finger Taps)

3 Reps

(Play and Count, Play and Chant, Block Positions and Patterns)

5 Challenges

("Joe's Song," Playing by Ear, Black-Key Improvisation)

More for Your Adult Method:

If you wish to play other pieces in different styles at each chapter level, look for the MORE FOR YOUR ADULT METHOD supplementary library at your local music store. The chart at the front of each book will help you determine which pieces fit with the levels in each chapter.

▌FACTS
Facts

FACTS define the musical concepts you need to know to play the PIECES BY CHOICE. You do not need to memorize them or fully understand each FACT the first time you encounter it. You will be referring back to the FACTS many times during upcoming lessons and will master them a little at a time.

Beat:
Music is organized by a steady heartbeat or pulse that creates a feeling of movement. Set a steady speed (tempo) and tap the following beats on a tabletop or on your knees.

| | | | | | | | | | | | | | |

Measures and Barlines:
Barlines group beats into measures for easier reading. Each measure contains a certain number of beats, or pulses. Set a steady tempo and tap the following beats as you read four pulses per measure.

| | | | | | | | | | | | | | | | | |

Sitting at the Piano

Sit comfortably with both feet on the floor.
Keep your elbows level with the keys of the piano.
Keep your forearms parallel with the floor.
Sit tall, but stay relaxed.

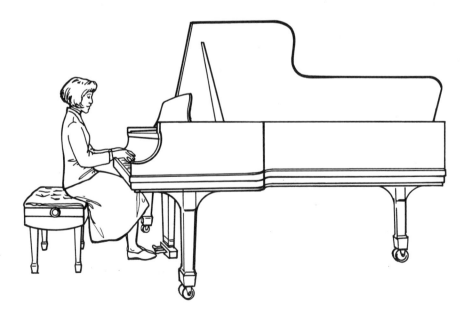

Notes and Rests:

Time values in music are symbolized by NOTES (for sound) and RESTS (for silence). Three common note and rest values are listed below, followed by the number of beats each receives and how to count the pulses.

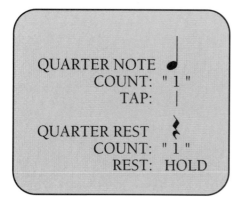

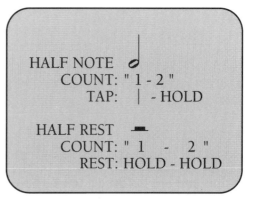

```
WHOLE NOTE    o
      COUNT: " 1  -  2  -  3  -  4 "
        TAP:  |  - HOLD - HOLD - HOLD

WHOLE REST    ▬
      COUNT: " 1  -  2  -  3  -  4 "
       REST: HOLD - HOLD - HOLD - HOLD
```

Repeat:

A REPEAT sign is two dots before a double bar. It means to play again.

Hand Position:

Let your arms hang comfortably and relaxed at your sides. Observe the shape of your hands. Are they gently curved and rounded, similar to the picture below?

Imagine that you are holding a tennis ball or a racquet ball in each hand. Keep your arms and hands relaxed as you lift and turn them to place the ball on a table top, as in the picture below.

Look closely at the picture of the hand position you will use in playing the piano. When you are playing, keep your fingers close to the surface of the keys. Keep your hands and fingers "shaped," but not "frozen," in this position.

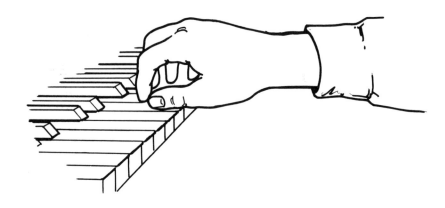

Fingering:

In piano playing, fingers are numbered as follows.

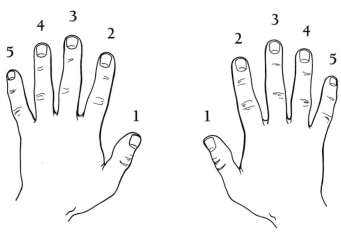

Place the palms of both hands together. Observe that ones are touching, twos are touching, threes are touching, fours are touching, and fives are touching.

Keyboard Direction:

LOWER (down) is to the LEFT. HIGHER (up) is to the RIGHT. The piano keyboard is laid out in patterns of black and white keys. Observe the repeated patterns of two black keys and three black keys.

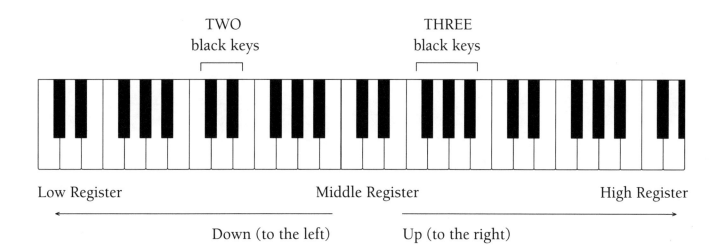

TWO
black keys

THREE
black keys

Low Register   Middle Register   High Register

Down (to the left)   Up (to the right)

FACTS

𝄞 Treble Clef:

This sign indicates that you will play keys in the MIDDLE and HIGH registers of the piano. The right hand usually plays notes written in the treble clef.

𝄢 Bass Clef:

This sign indicates that you will play in the MIDDLE and LOW registers of the piano. The left hand usually plays notes written in the bass clef.

Dynamics:

In music the relative loudness or softness of sound is referred to as dynamics. Dynamics are essential in playing expressively, shaping phrases, and communicating the intensity of the music. At the piano, when more weight is used to play, the sound will be louder. When less weight is used, the sound will be softer.

Dynamic markings are traditionally written in Italian. Three of the most common markings and their meanings are shown below.

f (forte) = LOUD

p (piano) = SOFT

mf (mezzo forte) = MODERATELY LOUD

Preps

PREPS relate to the FACTS and provide shortcuts to learning the PIECES BY CHOICE presented in the pull-out section of the book. The PREPS will develop your reading and technical abilities and help you build a secure musical foundation. In each chapter practice all PREPS in order to acquire all the skills and knowledge you will need in further chapters.

Tap and Count:

Read the following rhythm pattern. Feel the basic quarter-note pulse before you begin. Tap once for each note and count the appropriate number of beats aloud, as indicated.

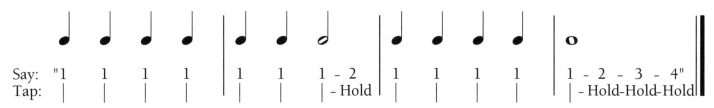

Repeat: Tap and count again, using the other hand.

 DISK/TAPE/CD LOGO
When this logo appears beside a PREP, REP, PIECE BY CHOICE or CHALLENGE, it indicates that a background accompaniment is available to accompany the activity.

Tap and Count:

Scan the following rhythm pattern. Feel the basic quarter-note pulse before you begin. Tap and count aloud.

Repeat: Tap and count again, using the other hand.

PREPS

Lap Taps:

"Joe's Song" page 2.

Tap the following rhythm pattern on your knee with your right hand. Count aloud the pulses appropriate to each note as practiced in the TAP and COUNT section. Repeat this PREP using the left hand and left knee.

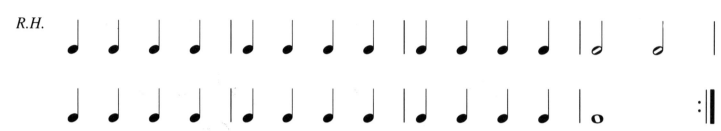

"Who's That?" page 3.

Tap the following rhythm pattern several times. The right hand taps the rhythm above the line. The left hand taps the rhythm below the line. When one hand is tapping, the other hand is resting. Keep the beat steady and continuous as you move from measure to measure.

Finger Taps:

The first two PREPS relate to "Joe's Song" and the third applies to "Who's That?" Tap individual fingers in the indicated hand. Use steady quarter notes if no rhythm is indicated. Chant the finger numbers in rhythm as you tap.

• "Joe's Song" page 2.

R.H. alone - 1 2 3 4 5 4 3 2 1 2 3 4 5

• *L.H.* alone - same pattern as above

• "Who's That?" page 3.

R.H.	—	3 4 3 2	—	3 4 2-HOLD
L.H.	5-HOLD 1-HOLD	—	5-HOLD 1-HOLD	—

Reps

Repeat the REPS every day, every practice period, even when you think you don't need them. They provide the backbone and the supportive structure for your current, and future progress. It is also advisable to review the FACTS and PREPS, because the skills you master studying and practicing those sections will help you play the PIECES BY CHOICE.

 ## Tap and Count:

"Joe's Song" page 2.

Tap this variation of "Joe's Song" with your left hand and count the pulses as you play. This melody will be the reverse of the original right-hand melody.

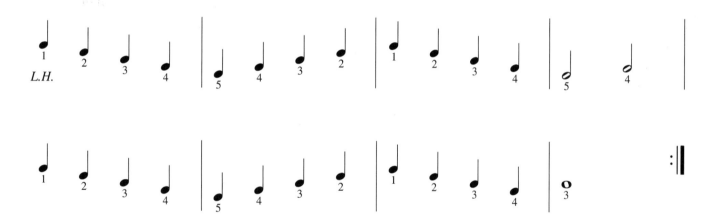

 ## Play and Chant:

"Joe's Song" page 2.

Play "Joe's Song" with your left hand while you chant the new finger numbers. Feel the beat. This melody will sound the same as the original right-hand melody.

L.H. 5 4 3 2 1 2 3 4 5 4 3 2 1 2

5 4 3 2 1 2 3 4 5 4 3 2 3

▛REPS

◎ Block Positions and Patterns:
"Who's That?" page 3.

A quick way to learn a piece is to play all the notes in a measure at the same time by blocking it. Playing in block position allows you to feel secure within the overall shape of the music. Blocking also prepares you to play individual notes with individual fingers more easily.

- To block the left hand, play fingers 5 and 1 at the same time. Play the left-hand block and hold it for four counts (one whole measure).

- To block the right hand, play fingers 4, 3 and 2 at the same time. Play the right-hand block and hold it for four counts (one full measure).

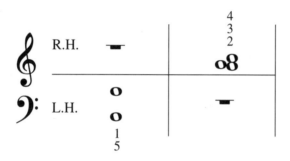

- Play "Who's That?" in block positions. Play the block position on count one of each measure and hold for a total of four counts. You will continue to alternate L R L R L R L R, as written.

- Exchange parts by playing the original left-hand part with the right hand in the upper register and by playing the original right-hand part with the left hand in the middle register, as in the excerpt below. You may need to write out a complete fingering chart for this REP.

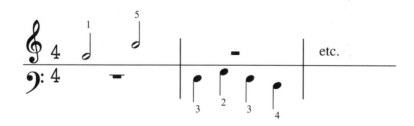

CHALLENGES

Challenges

These additional options and practice suggestions are either more difficult than PREPS and REPS, or present different musical experiences related to the FACTS of the chapter. You may choose all, some, or none of these CHALLENGES.

 "Joe's Song" page 2.

VARIATION I: Place your left hand in position to play the piece (5 and 4 on two black keys; 3, 2, and 1 on three black keys). Keep the rhythm the same as the original. Change the melody by playing the following finger numbers. (They are actually the same as the original right-hand finger numbers.)

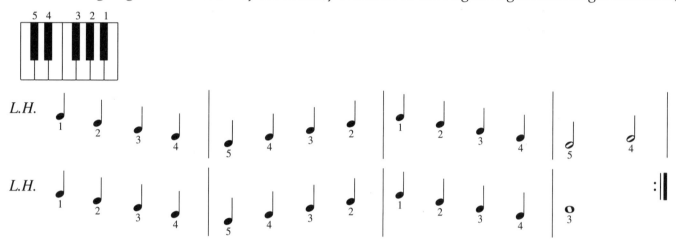

VARIATION II PARALLEL MOTION: Play "Joe's Song" with both hands.

VARIATION III CONTRARY MOTION: Play "Joe's Song" in the right hand while the left hand plays "Joe's Song," Variation I at the same time. This is playing in CONTRARY MOTION.

Playing by Ear:

The following four melodies can be played on black keys only. After choosing one of the titles, remind yourself of the melody, try to find the starting note, and play the tune. You will discover that some of the keys you will need to play occur outside of one hand position. Experiment with various fingerings until you find one that works for you. Play the melody with your other hand in the middle register of the keyboard.

"Amazing Grace"
"Auld Lang Syne"
"I'd Like To Teach the World to Sing"
"Swing Low, Sweet Chariot"

15

CHALLENGES

⚙ Black-Key Improvisation:

There are no mistakes in improvisation; however, some choices are better than others! In this particular activity any black key will sound good as a melody note.

Black-Key Position:

Choose any group of black keys for your hand position and get ready to play.

Listen

Listen as the Disk/CD/Tape or your teacher plays the accompaniment below and feel the pulse of the music.

Improvise

Improvise a melody made up of quarter notes and half notes. Play in the upper or middle ranges of the piano using black keys only. Use your right hand for a while and then use your left hand.

Dynamics

As the Disk/CD/Tape varies the dynamics, play your melody to match the loudness or softness of the accompaniment.

The End

Plan the ending so that the melody either ends and allows the accompaniment to conclude the improvisation; or, the accompaniment ends while you provide a brief, but expressive, fade out in the melody.

Accompaniment
Flowing

(vary) *mf*

CHAPTER 2 : Piano Basics & White Keys

Pieces No Choice
("Jacob's Alphabet," "Alphabet Ballad," "Take C") pages 4 & 5.

Pieces By Choice

"Ode To Joy" page 6.

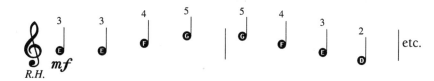

"Love Me Tender" page 7.

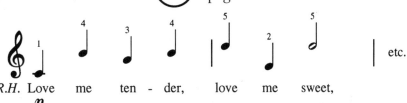

"When The Saints Go Marching In" page 8.

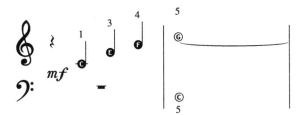

18 Facts
(Musical Alphabet, Direction and Distance, Notation: dotted-half note and tie)

20 Preps
(White-Key Groups, Block Positions, Observe, Eyes Closed, Lap Taps: "Jacob's Alphabet," Finger Taps: "Alphabet Ballad," "Take C")

24 Reps
(Finger Taps, Mirrored Pattern, Directional Reading, Lap Taps)

28 Challenges
("Jacob's Alphabet," "Ode To Joy," Listening, "Love Me Tender," "When The Saints Go Marching In")

Musical Alphabet:

Music uses the first seven letters of the alphabet for naming the white keys on the piano. Sets of seven letters, A-B-C-D-E-F-G, repeat over the entire keyboard. Use a pencil and circle the alphabetical sets of white keys, A-G.

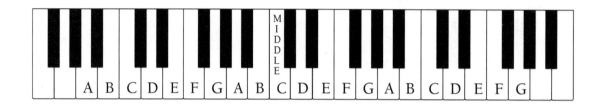

Direction and Distance:

Higher

Use your third finger to play the white keys, from A to G, in a steady rhythm, moving higher (forward in the alphabet). Name each key as you play it. Do the same, using the other hand.

HIGHER

Lower

Use your third finger to play the white keys, from G to A, in a steady rhythm, moving lower (backward in the alphabet). Name each key as you play it. Do the same, using the other hand.

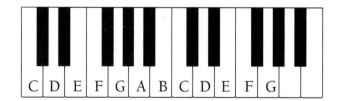

LOWER

Steps

Alphabetical movement from one white key to another, up or down, is by STEP. Moving higher and lower alphabetically is an example of moving by STEP. Music reading requires that you be able to start on any key and move by step in either direction.

STEPPING UP: Play and name white keys, A-B-C-D-E-F-G.

STEPPING DOWN: Play and name white keys, G-F-E-D-C-B-A.

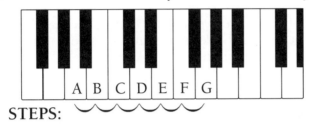

STEPS:

Skips

Movement that plays one white key, skips one white key, and plays the next (up or down) is called a SKIP. Music reading requires that you be able to start on any key and move by skip in either direction. Practice naming and playing white keys that move by skip, up and down the keyboard.

SKIPPING UP: Play and name white keys, A-C-E-G-B-D-F.

SKIPPING DOWN: Play and name white keys, F-D-B-G-E-C-A.

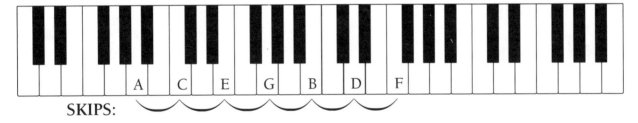

SKIPS:

Notation: Dotted-Half Note and Tie

DOT - A dot increases the time value of a note by half of that note's value.

DOTTED-HALF NOTE 𝅗𝅥.
    COUNT: "1 - 2 - 3"
    TAP: | - Hold - Hold

TIE - A curved line that connects two successive notes of the same pitch asks you to hold ONE SOUND for the combined duration of the tied notes.

COUNT: "1 - 2 - Tie - 2" = "1 - 2 - 3 - 4"
TAP: | - Hold - Tie - Hold = | - Hold - Hold - Hold

2 PREPS

Preps

In each chapter practice all PREPS in order to acquire the skills and knowledge you will need in further chapters.

White-Key Groups:

The names and locations of white keys are easily recognized by their positions relative to the groups of two and three black keys. For example, the CDE group of white keys surrounds the two black keys, while the FGAB group of white keys surrounds the three black keys.

Block Positions:

The C Group

Using the right hand, fingers 1-2-3, block the CDE group in several locations on the keyboard. Do the same with the left hand, using fingers 3-2-1.

L.H: 3   2   1

The F Group

Using the right hand, fingers 1-2-3-4, block the FGAB group in several locations on the keyboard.
Do the same with the left hand, using fingers 4-3-2-1.

R.H.: 1   2   3   4

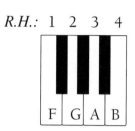

L.H.: 4   3   2   1

Observe:

- C is always to the left of TWO black keys; D is in the middle; E is on the right.
- F is always to the left of THREE black keys; B is to the right; G and A are in between.

Eyes Closed:

- Sweep your hands up and down the black keys. Feel the groups of twos and threes.
- Relative to two black keys - play a C; play a D; play an E.
  Do the same in the other hand.

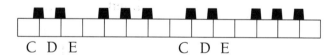

- Relative to three black keys - play an F; play a B; play G and A.
  Do the same in the other hand.

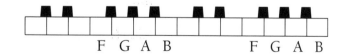

- Retain this mental IMPRINT of the keyboard layout.

 PREPS

 Lap Taps:

"Jacob's Alphabet" page 4.

• Tap the following rhythm pattern with one hand. As you tap, chant the music alphabet "A B C D E F G." Repeat the pattern several times with each hand.

```
A    B    C    D    E    F    G    -    A    B    C    D    E    F    G    -
```

Now you are ready to play "Jacob's Alphabet." You may use any finger you choose, however, the third finger is recommended for best balance.

"Alphabet Ballad" page 4.

• Tap and count the following rhythm pattern several times with each hand.

Use the above rhythm pattern to tap and chant the music alphabet several times- forward (A B C D E F G--) and backward (G F E D C B A--). Now you are ready to play "Alphabet Ballad."

"Take C" page 5.
- Tap and count the following rhythm pattern several times using the indicated hands.

R.H. ♩♩♩ | ♩♩♩ | — — | — — | ♩♩♩ | ♩♩♩ | — | o ‖

L.H. — | — | ♪♪♪♪ ♪♪♪♪ | — — | — — | ♪♪♪♪ | — ‖

Finger Taps:

"Take C"

- Tap individual fingers in the indicated hand. Chant individual fingers in the indicated hand.

R.H.	1 2 3 –	1 2 3 –	—	—	1 2 3 –	1 2 3 –	—	1– – –
L.H.	—	—	4 3 2 1	4 3 2 1	—	—	4 3 2 1	—

- Turn to "Take C" and tap finger numbers as you did above, but this time chant the indicated letter names. You are now ready to read and play "Take C."

REPS

Reps

REPS are to be repeated every day, every practice period, even when you think you don't need them. Also, review FACTS and PREPS.

◉ Finger Taps:

"Take C" page 5.

Tap individual fingers in the indicated hand while chanting finger numbers in rhythm as you tap.

R.H.	1 2 3 —	1 2 3 —	▬	▬	1 2 3 —	1 2 3 —	▬	1 — — —
L.H.	▬	▬	4 3 2 1	4 3 2 1	▬	▬	4 3 2 1	▬

◉ Mirrored Pattern:

"E, I Know"

The pattern below is almost a mirror of "Take C." The notes move the same distance, but in the opposite direction. "E, I Know," which follows, uses the mirrored pattern.

- Tap finger numbers as you did above, but this time chant letter names.

R.H.	E D C —	E D C —	▬	▬	
L.H.	▬	▬	B A G F	B A G F	etc.

- Play "E, I Know" on the piano. It can be played with the same disk/CD/tape accompaniment as "Take C."

Directional Reading:

"E, I Know"

• Read "E, I Know" by direction. Chant the following, while you play:

"E, down, down -, E, down, down -, B, down, down, down, B, down, down, down,
E, down, down -, E, down, down -, B, down, down, B, C---."

• When you say "down," you are acknowledging that the melody moves down by step.

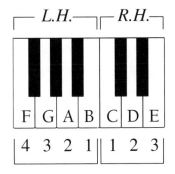

E, I Know

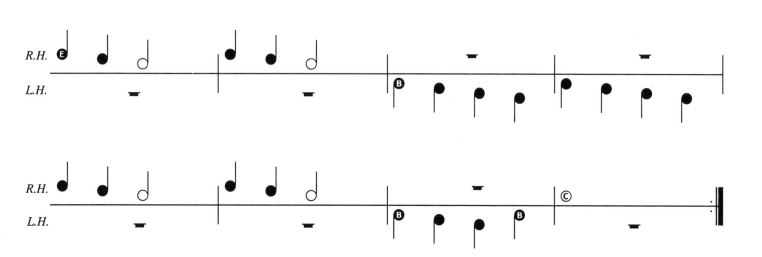

REPS

"Take C"   page 5.

- Read "Take C" aloud, similiar to the way you read "E, I Know:" "C, up, up-, C, up, up-."
Finish reading the piece in this manner, chanting the direction of the pitches.

"Ode To Joy"   page 6.

- Read "Ode to Joy" by direction. When a note repeats in the melody, say "same."

- Tap and say the finger numbers of measures 1-4 with the right hand. Tap and say the finger numbers of measures 5-8 with the left hand.

- Tap the finger numbers for all eight measures while chanting the letter names of the white keys.

- Place both hands in position on the piano. Establish a steady beat, and play.

"Love Me Tender"   page 7.

- Write out the fingering chart for the left-hand melody.

  L.H.   5   2   3   2   1   4   1 —   etc.

- Teach your left hand to play "Love Me Tender."

 Lap Taps:

These tap and count REPS will greatly shorten the learning time and the frustration that sometimes occurs when you attempt to play fingers, notes, and rhythms in two hands at the same time. Remember, you also want to build overall skill while you are learning each piece.

"When The Saints Go Marching In" page 8.

Tap and count the following rhythm pattern several times in these ways.

- Right hand alone, counting pulses (including rests and ties) aloud.
- Left hand alone, counting pulses aloud.
- Hands together, counting the right-hand part while you tap both.

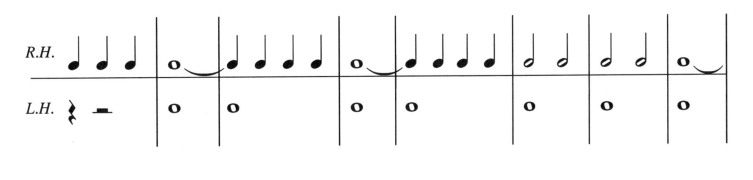

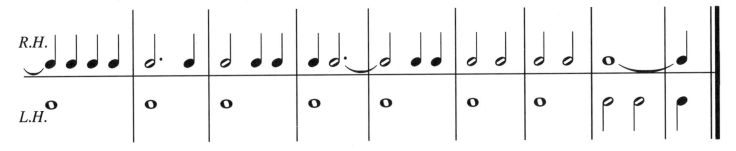

2 CHALLENGES

Challenges

These additional options and practice suggestions are either more difficult than PREPS and REPS, or present different musical experiences related to the FACTS of the chapter. You may choose all, some, or none of these CHALLENGES.

 "Jacob's Alphabet" (descending): page 4.

Reverse the melody by playing the music alphabet backward, G F E D C B A -.
• Begin with the highest G on your piano and play three descending sets of the music alphabet.

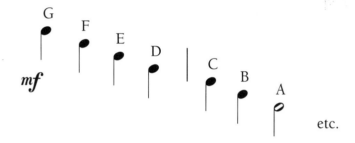

 "Ode To Joy" page 6.

Play the melody in the following ways.

• Right hand only, all eight measures.
• Left hand only, all eight measures. Write out the fingering if you need to.
• Both hands together, parallel motion throughout.

Listening:

"Ode to Joy" is the theme from the last movement of Beethoven's Ninth Symphony. Listen to a recording of the original setting of this tune. It also appears in many hymnals as, "Joyful, Joyful, We Adore Thee."

 "Love Me Tender" (PIECES BY CHOICE) page 7.

- Write the appropriate letter name *under* each note of the melody.

- Play the melody in both hands at the same time (parallel motion) while the disk/CD/tape or your teacher plays the accompaniment.

"When The Saints Go Marching In" (PIECES BY CHOICE) page 8.

- Play the left hand alone while you sing (whistle, hum, or "think") the melody.
- Teach your left hand to play the melody. Write a fingering chart for the left hand.

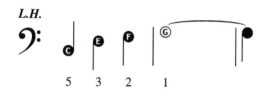

- Use a sequencer or a tape recorder to record the right-hand part. Then, you can play the left-hand part with the recorded right hand, or record both, *a la* recording studio.

White-Key Improvisation:

- Remember, there are no mistakes in improvisation; however, some choices are better than others. In this particular activity any white key will sound good as a melody note. Review the instructions given for Black-Key Improvisation on page 16 and apply them to improvisation on the white keys.

Accompaniment

Moderately fast

CHAPTER : Staff, Intervals, & Meter

Pieces No Choice

("You'll Be All Right," "Teddy's Tune")   pages 9 & 10.

Pieces By Choice

"Ode To Joy"   page 12.

etc.

"When The Saints Go Marching In"   page 13.

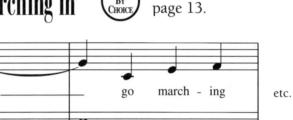

etc.

"Color Wheel"   page 14.

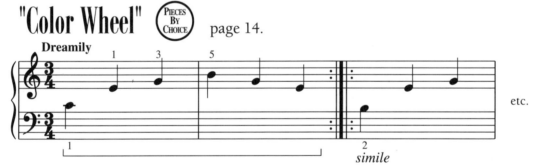

etc.

The Staff:

The staff consists of five lines and four spaces. Notes on a staff can be line notes or space notes.

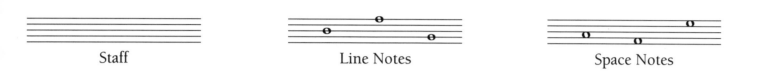

Staff   Line Notes   Space Notes

Treble and Bass Clef Signs:

Staff reading requires you to relate specific notes on the staff to specific keys on the piano. The TREBLE CLEF SIGN (also called the G clef sign) identifies the G above middle C and locates it on the second line of the treble staff. THE BASS CLEF SIGN (also called the F clef sign) identifies the F below middle C and locates it on the fourth line of the bass staff.

Treble G   Bass F

Grand Staff:

The grand staff unites the TREBLE staff and BASS staff.

Reading Guides:

Three important READING GUIDES act as references for naming all other lines and spaces: MIDDLE C, TREBLE G, AND BASS F. Middle C on the keyboard sits precisely in the "middle" between bass F (two skips down from C) and treble G (two skips up from C). On the staff, middle C sits on a LEDGER LINE, either directly above the bass staff, or directly below the treble staff. Visually, middle C does not appear to be "in the middle," but on the piano keyboard and on the staff, it is in the middle of bass F and treble G.

Reading Guides:

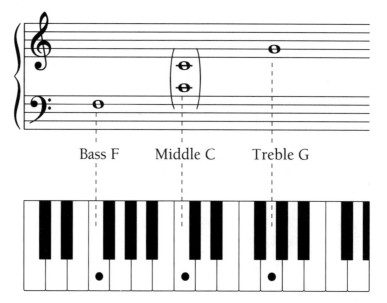

The Grand Staff:

Notes on the GRAND STAFF are named alphabetically as they ascend, alternating line-space-line-space, etc.

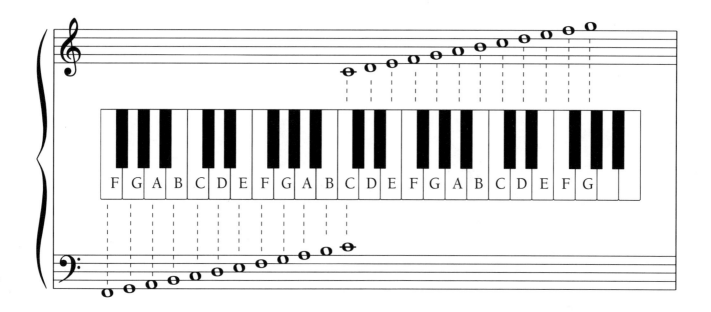

Intervals:

Intervals denote the alphabetical distance between notes.

SECOND
  - The interval of a SECOND occurs when two notes are adjacent alphabetically and appear on a line and in the very next space, or in a space and on the very next line, in either direction. To play a SECOND, step up or down to the next finger. Movement by SECONDS is stepwise.

THIRD
  - The interval of a THIRD occurs when two notes appear on two consecutive lines or two consecutive spaces, in either direction. To play a THIRD, SKIP a finger. Movement by SKIP is a THIRD.

Seconds   Thirds

Ledger Lines:

These short lines are added ABOVE, BELOW, or in the MIDDLE of the grand staff to extend the range of the treble and bass clefs. Memorize the A-C-E groups involving ledger lines and their locations on the grand staff. The A-C-E groups illustrated below are easily recognizable because they occur on three consecutive lines.

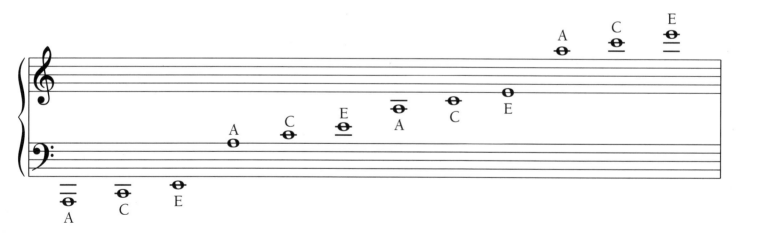

Meter Signature (Time Signature):

This sign appears at the beginning of each composition. The top number indicates the pulses (or beats) in a measure. The bottom number of the meter signature indicates the type of note value that will receive one pulse.

- A **2/4** meter signature indicates "two beats per measure;" a quarter note gets one pulse. Identify the meanings of **3/4** and **4/4** meter signatures. The symbol "C" means "common time," **4/4**, and is sometimes used in place of a numerical meter signature.

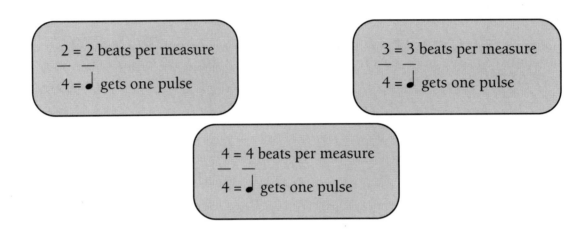

- Prior to now, all of the counting you have done has been with pulse. Meter signatures let you know the placement of the beat in each measure, enabling you to count in an additional way. The counting system below communicates pulse and position in the measure.

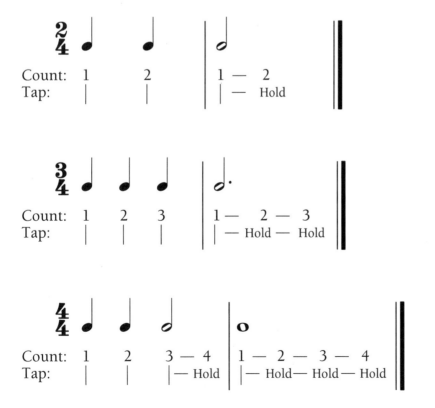

Measures (Complete and Incomplete):

In all music writing, the total time value of the notes in each measure must be exact and complete. The only exception to that rule may occur at the very beginning of a piece of music.

- Sometimes an incomplete measure, one or more UPBEATS, occurs before the first complete measure. The time value of this incomplete measure is usually subtracted from the final measure, making it also incomplete.

Damper Pedal:

Pianos may have one, two, or three pedals. Regardless of the number of pedals on your instrument, the damper pedal will be the one on the right. When you hold it down, tones on the piano will continue to sound after you release the keys.

- Use the damper pedal with your right foot and keep your heel anchored to the floor, similar to using the gas pedal in a car. Pedal markings are as follows.

PEDALS:

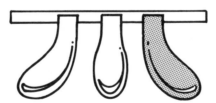

Down   Hold   Up

- "Color Wheel," on page 14 uses the damper pedal. Practice using the pedal when you learn this piece.

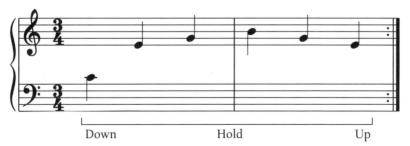

Down   Hold   Up

3 PREPS

Preps

Pianists who read music fluently possess a great asset. Fluent reading makes learning time much shorter, progress greater, and frustration less frequent. Successful reading and playing happens when hands and fingers coordinate with each other. PREPS will emphasize the connection between reading and coordination. Some PREPS will help increase your general reading ability and some will directly prepare you to play the choice selections. Prepare, play, and enjoy.

Tap and Count:

- Left hand alone, right hand alone, and hands together = L, R, TOG. Count the quarter-note pulse, then repeat, counting the meter.

- Use your right hand to tap the notes with stems up and your left hand to tap notes with the stems down.

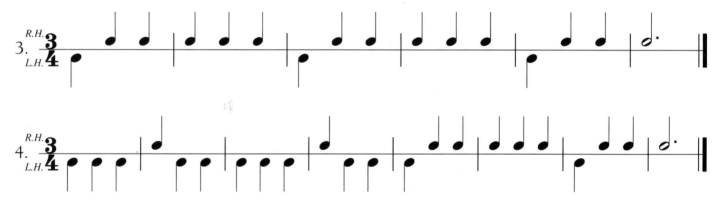

Finger Taps:

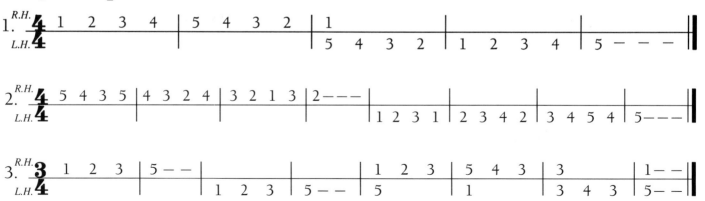

Staff Reading:

The following section provides brief melodies for reading. Your reading system combines rhythm and intervals (direction and distance), using the READING GUIDES on the staff - Treble G, Bass F, and Middle C. To learn to read, use each of the following steps faithfully. Your work will pay off in a big way if you do.

Tap and Count

Practice each melody two ways: the first time chanting pulse and the second time counting meter. Be sure to tap with the same hand that will eventually play the melody.

Tap and Verbalize Intervals (direction and distance):

When reading SECONDS, say either "up," or "down." (It is not necessary to say "up a second" when you recognize the line-space or space-line relationship.) For example, in Melody 1, you would say, "G, down, down, down, down, up, up, up, up. For Melody 8, you would say, "G, down a third, up, down a third, up, down a third."

Finger Taps with Finger Numbers

Using the hand that will play the melody, tap each finger as you say its NUMBER. Repeat, saying the LETTER NAMES of notes.

Play

Play each melody three times on the keyboard, verbalizing letter names, intervals, and finger numbers on each repetition. Keep your eyes on the music. After you have found the position on the keyboard, DO NOT LOOK DOWN while you play.

3 PREPS

Staff Reading

⟫ Read and Play:

The next two pieces will give you additional reading practice within a lengthier composition. Use the reading steps listed in the STAFF READING in PREPS 3 on page 37 to help you learn rapidly. Be sure to play each piece as a duet with a partner or with the Disk/CD/Tape.

"You'll Be All Right" page 9.

- Place your right hand on the white keys A-B-C-D-E. Start at the top of your hand position and play "5, down, down, down a third." Those are the notes in the first two measures.

- Shift your entire hand position down one white key to G-A-B-C-D. Start at the top and play the same pattern of intervals as in the first two measures. Keep moving down and playing the two measure pattern two more times.

- Measure 9 is like the beginning, but watch out for the ending. The last two measures (the fourth pattern) are different. Are you frustrated? You'll Be All Right!

"Teddy's Tune" page 10.

- This piece is played with both hands in the C Position. Be sure to practice reading direction and distance.

- Notice patterns of notes, such as the one found in the first measure - G, down, down, up a third. That pattern is repeated on F, and on E, in the next two measures.

- Can you find other patterns to facilitate your reading of new music? Prepare the last two measures: parallel motion.

REPS

Reps

Remember, REPS (repetitions) are for practice every day. Review FACTS and PREPS as needed.

Warm-ups:

Refer to the three FINGER TAPS in PREPS 3, page 36. Play these finger taps on the piano using the C Position. Experiment with the sounds of other five-note hand positions.

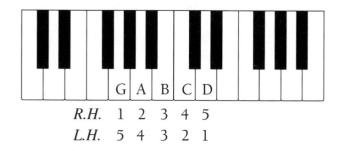

| | R.H. | 1 | 2 | 3 | 4 | 5 |
| | L.H. | 5 | 4 | 3 | 2 | 1 |

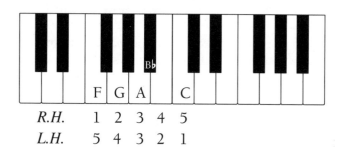

| | R.H. | 1 | 2 | 3 | 4 | 5 |
| | L.H. | 5 | 4 | 3 | 2 | 1 |

Blocking:

"You'll Be All Right" page 9.

In the right hand, practice blocking the first and last note of each two-measure pattern. Play each BLOCK, holding it for 8 counts. Notice the top note of each BLOCK and how it moves from one position to the next.

play as

Challenges

You may choose all, some, or none of these CHALLENGES.

Staff Reading:

Refer to the STAFF READING on page 38 and play melodies 1-8 as written. Teach the left hand to play melodies 1-4, and teach the right hand to play melodies 5-8. When doing this particular challenge, do not read letter names on the staff; read starting note, intervals and direction. You may also choose to double the melodies by playing them in both hands at the same time, parallel motion.

Melody 1 Play one octave lower than written.   Melody 5

"You'll Be All Right"   (PIECES BY CHOICE)   page 9.

Teach your left hand to play "You'll Be All Right." Can you play both hands at the same time? Write out a fingering chart for measures 13-16, each hand.

```
             13
R.H.    5    4    3    1 |  etc.
             13
L.H.    1    2    3    5 |  etc.
```

"Ode To Joy"   (PIECES BY CHOICE)   page 12.

Play measures 1-4 in the bass clef, with your left hand. Play measures 5-8 in the treble clef, with your right hand.

3 CHALLENGES

Rhythm Section:

Use a drum, cymbal, brushes, sand blocks, or other rhythm instruments to create a percussion part to accompany "When the Saints Go Marching In," "Color Wheel," "White-Key Improvisation," page 29, "Black-Key Improvisation" page 16, or any other appropriate pieces. (If percussion instruments are not available, use kitchen utensils, keys and other "found objects" around the house.) Use a sequencer or tape recorder to prepare your own "play along" tape.

Black-Key Improvisation:

- Listen to the accompaniment on the Disk/CD/Tape, or as played by your teacher. Identify the pulse, the meter, and the mood of the music. Imagine a style of melody that would sound good with the accompaniment.

- Improvise a melody using only black keys. You may wish to follow the suggested rhythm pattern below in improvising your melody.

- Shape phrases and don't forget to improvise occasionally with your other hand.

Accompaniment:

CHAPTER 4: Major Keys & Triads

Pieces No Choice
("It Was Almost Like A Song," "Sun Of My Soul," "Restless Night") pages 37, 15, & 16.

Pieces By Choice

"Largo" page 18.

"Kum-Ba-Yah" page 19.

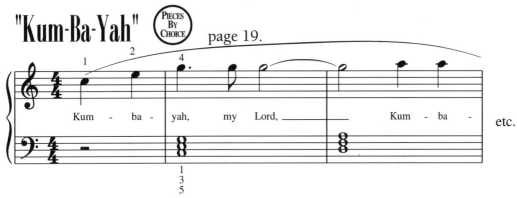

Kum - ba - yah, my Lord, _____ _____ Kum - ba - etc.

ACTS

Major Keys and Scales:

A piece of music is "in the key of C," when most, or sometimes all, of the tones in that piece are taken from the C MAJOR SCALE and the tonal center is C, the key note. A major scale can be built on any starting note by following the same specific order of half and whole steps as found in the Appendix under MAJOR SCALES, page 104.

Whole and Half Steps:

- A HALF STEP on the piano is the distance from one key to the very next key, black or white; higher or lower. It is the smallest possible distance on the keyboard. HALF STEPS can occur between a black and a white key, or between two sets of white keys (E and F, B and C).
- A WHOLE STEP is the combination of two consecutive HALF STEPS.

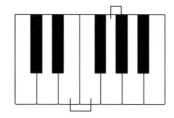   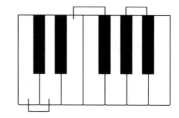

HALF STEP: From one key   WHOLE STEP: Two half steps.
to the next, black or white.

Accidentals:

SHARPS, FLATS, and NATURALS are music symbols that temporarily alter the pitch of notes by a HALF STEP. Accidentals are written on the staff and apply to the note immediately following the symbol. The effect of an accidental continues throughout the remainder of the measure and affects only the measure in which it appears.

- A SHARP (♯) raises a note one half step. When you see it, play the next key to the right, black or white.
- A FLAT (♭) lowers a note one half step. When you see it, play the next key to the left, black or white.
- A NATURAL (♮) cancels a sharp or a flat.
- CHROMATIC movement occurs when tones move by half step, such as G, G♯, A.

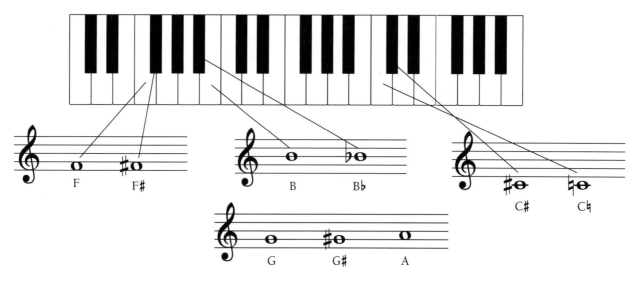

Chromatic Movement

Major Triad:

A major triad, or CHORD, is made up of tones 1 (root), 3, and 5 of a major scale. Three of the most commonly used major chords and their related scales are shown below. (See the Appendix for additional information regarding chords and scales.)

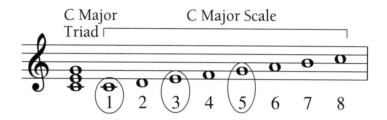

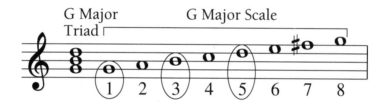

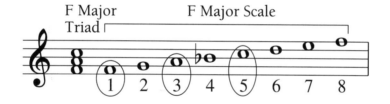

 # FACTS

Major Five-Finger Pattern:

A major five-finger pattern is made up of the first five notes of a major scale. All major five-finger patterns are played with fingers 5-4-3-2-1 in the left hand, and with fingers 1-2-3-4-5 in the right hand. This hand position outlines the major triad and is one of the most basic shapes for all piano playing. All major five-finger patterns appear in the Appendix, page 103. The major patterns for C, F, and G are notated below.

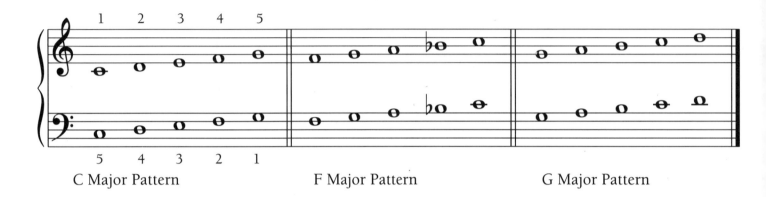

C Major Pattern   F Major Pattern   G Major Pattern

Intervals:

Fifth

Triads are built in thirds (line-line-line, or space-space-space). When spelling triads, begin with the root and go up a third, up a third (root-3rd-5th).

- The distance between the root and the middle note of a triad is a THIRD. The distance between the root and the top note of a triad is a FIFTH. Within a five-finger position, a FIFTH is played between fingers 1 and 5.

- Play the following fifths beginning on C:

- Do the same with G as the root; with F as the root.

Broken and Blocked Intervals

Broken and blocked refers to the vertical and horizontal ways in which notes are written on the staff and to the way they sound when played. Broken intervals sound separately, MELODICALLY. Blocked intervals sound together, HARMONICALLY. Root position triads are fingered, right hand - 1 3 5; left hand - 5 3 1.

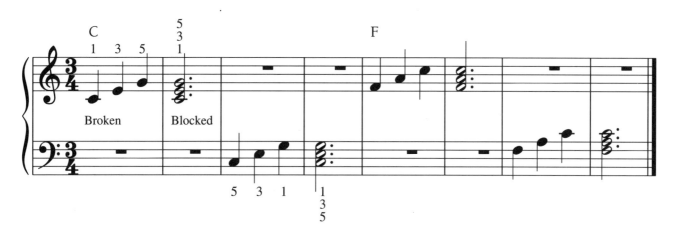

FACTS

Notation: Eighth Notes, Eighth Rests, and Dotted-Quarter Notes

Pairs (or larger groups) of eighth notes are often connected with a beam, while individual eighth notes have flags. Remember, when a dot is added to a note, it increases the length of the note by one half of the note's value.

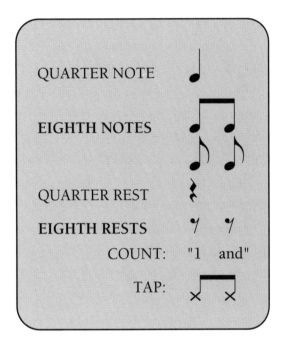

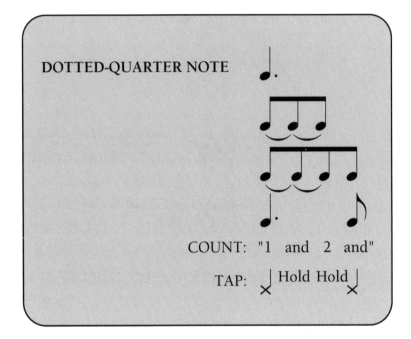

Slur:

A slur is a curved line over or under a group of notes, indicating that those notes should be played LEGATO (smooth and connected). Slurs are also used to indicate phrases in music. Notice the difference between ties and slurs in the example below.

"Kum-Ba-Yah"

Sequence:

A sequence is the repetition of a pattern of notes at different pitch levels. The ability to recognize sequential patterns in music will ensure fluent and rapid learning. The patterns may involve fingerings, harmonies, melodies, or all three.

SEQUENCES: 1.   1 - 2 - 3, 2 - 3 - 4, 3 - 4 - 5, and so on.

2.

3.

Lead Line:

A LEAD LINE of a song consists of the melody, the lyrics (if any), and the chord symbols written in letters above the tune. FAKE BOOKS contain lead lines for large numbers of songs and from these essential outlines, a performer can create an "arrangement," or improvise ("fake") an accompaniment. In this chapter we will begin to learn some of the skills necessary to read lead lines.

Comping:

Comping is one of the skills related to lead line reading. In musical slang it means to "accompany" while the melody is played or sung by someone else. The following exerpt is presented to illustrate the overall "look" of lead lines and comp harmonies. You are not expected to play this example at this time.

Lead line sample: "It Was Almost Like A Song"

Comp sample (bass/chord style):

4 PREPS

Preps

It's that time again! Prepare, read, play, and get coordinated.

◎ Tap and Count

(L, R, TOG = L.H., R.H., and Hands Together. Count with pulse, then repeat, counting with meter.)

1.

2.

3.

4.

5.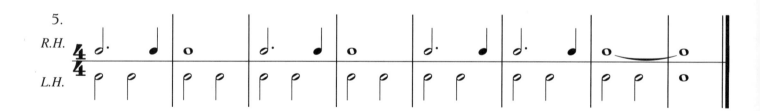

6.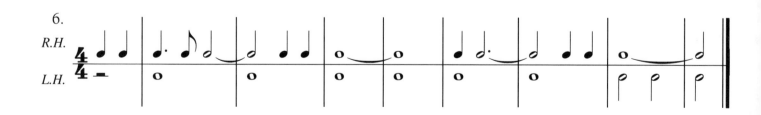

Finger Taps:

1.
```
4  5 4 3 2 | 1 2 3 4 | 5       |         | 1 - 3 - | 5 - 3 - | 1 - 5 - | 1 - - - ‖
4          |         | 1 2 3 4 | 5 4 3 2 | 1 - 3 - | 5 - 3 - | 1 - 5 - | 1 - - - ‖
```

2.
```
4  1 2 3 4 | 5 4 3 2 | 1 - - - | 1       |         5 |         | 1 - - - ‖
4  5       | 1       | 5 - - - | 5 4 3 2 | 1 2 3 4   | 5 - - - |         ‖
```

3.
```
3          |         | 1  2  1 |       | 5 5 5 | 4 - 2 | 3 2 1 |       ‖
4  1 1 1 | 1 2 1 |         | 1 - - |       |       |       | 1 - - ‖
```

Staff Reading:

The following section provides brief musical examples for staff reading. Remember to use the READING GUIDES (Treble G, Bass F, Middle C), direction and distance (intervals), and rhythm when preparing to read music.

It is not necessary to be "at the piano" every time you practice reading. Verbalize, tap, and count the examples on your desk or at the kitchen table as often as you play them on the piano. Follow the plan below and use it every time you read. In this section, you are reviewing how to read seconds and thirds, while practicing the newer concepts of fifths and hands together.

The more you choose to read, the faster you will progress.

Tap and Count Two ways: pulse and meter.

Tap Rhythm and Verbalize Intervals Direction and distance.

Finger Taps with Finger Numbers Repeat, saying letter names.

Play Do not look at your hands while they are playing these examples.

4PREPS

🔊 Read and Play:

The next three pieces will give you practice in reading outside the five-finger C position. You will still read by intervals, but you will use additional patterns and hand positions to help you. Fluent reading will be one of the greatest rewards of your piano study.

"It Was Almost Like A Song" page 37.

The following melody (LEAD LINE) is SEQUENTIAL. The right hand plays the same pattern of fingers (3 2 1 3 2) four times, beginning on Treble G and moving down one white key each time the pattern is played. The pattern occurs on G, on F, on E, and on D. The last time (on D) the rhythm is slightly different because of the lyric, the EXTRA two words, "It was." We will learn about the chords for this tune later. For now, concentrate on the sequences in the melody.

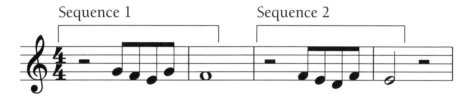

"Sun Of My Soul" page 15.

Place each hand in the indicated five finger-position, then read and play the melody by intervals while the Disk/CD/Tape plays the accompaniment. A few letter names have been written to help you when the tune moves from hand to hand. Otherwise, read the seconds and thirds as they move within each hand.

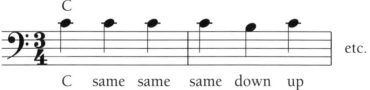

"Restless Night" page 16.

This piece uses both hands to play the two-measure patterns. Observe the following:

- The right hand always plays the pattern, 5 323 1, followed by the left hand playing a descending fifth, 1 5.
- The pattern repeats a step lower every two measures.
- Identify the accidentals in measures 7, 13, and 14.
- Block the first and last note of each measure to practice the positions.

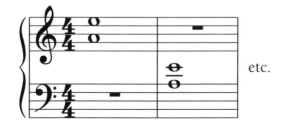

- First play the song as a solo and then as a duet with the Disk/CD/Tape or your teacher.

Extended Range:

Although the most basic hand position is the five-finger pattern, most songs and piano pieces you want to play will use movement beyond this limited five-note range. The following PIECES BY CHOICE present three instances where hands are required to shift outside of their starting positions to accomodate a wider range of notes.

"Largo" page 18.

Chromatic Movement

Chromatic movement occurs in measures 11 and 12 in the left hand: G G♯ A. Use fingers 1 2 1. Play G with 1; cross 2 over 1 to play G♯; then play A with 1.

Substitutions

On the last note in the example above, play G with 2 and replace the second finger with 1 while you continue holding. You have now played outside the five-note range and have returned your left hand to the C position in an orderly manner.

"Kum-Ba-Yah"  page 19.

Intervals Larger than a Fifth

In the right-hand part of "Kum-Ba-Yah," shown above, the range of notes goes beyond the fifth but all the intervals are either seconds, thirds, fifths, or repeats, all of which you know how to read. Good fingering habits will help you play LEGATO, as indicated by the slurs. Fingerings are marked only in places that are exceptions to the obvious. Follow the fingering as indicated in the music. Be consistent!

Root Position Triads

The left-hand part of "Kum-Ba-Yah" is made up of ROOT POSITION TRIADS. They are all line-line-line, or space-space-space. Play them all with fingering, 5 3 1. Practice the left hand separately. As you shift to a new chord, lead with the fifth finger.

"Welcome To My World" page 20.

Right-Hand Sequences

The quickest way to learn this song is to identify the sequences. In the right hand, play the first five notes. How many more times do you play that pattern? Where and how does it move?

Left-Hand Sequences

Find the three-note sequence in the left hand. In measures 8 and 9 and measures 16 and 17 the left hand moves differently.

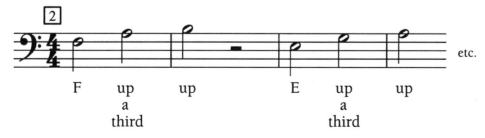

 # REPS

Reps

REPS guide your everyday practice and review. Regular practice that is dedicated and organized assures satisfying progress. Playing the piano needs mental and physical skills that require training, much the same as an athletic activity. If you observe the rules, practice, and do the necessary hard work, feelings of accomplishment and enjoyment will follow!

Warm-ups:

It is important to warm up your mind and your fingers at each practice session. Play the FINGER TAPS found in the PREPS 4 section (page 51) on the piano. Use white-key five-finger positions on C, F, and G.

Lap Taps and Fingertaps:

Practice both LAP TAPS and FINGERTAPS on all of the READ and PLAY pieces on page 52 and on the PIECES BY CHOICE in chapter four.

Blocking:

"Restless Night" page 16.

In measure 1, block fingers 5 3 1 in the right hand to create a chord. In measure 2, block the left hand fifth. Play right hand and left hand blocked, at the same time.

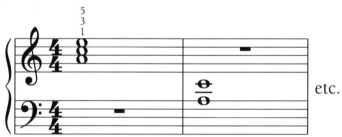

Do the same on measures 3 and 4, and so on. With the Disk/CD/Tape play "Restless Night" in blocked position holding each blocked position for eight counts.

"Welcome To My World" page 20.

Block and play each position of the right hand. Each position of the left hand has three notes in it. Block and play the left hand positions. These blocks will produce "clusters" of sound rather than pleasant sounding chords.

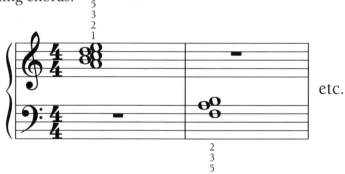

By blocking, you will feel secure about the hand shapes and will feel the overall positions for groups of notes. Play "Welcome To My World" in blocked position, holding each chord for four counts.

Shortcuts:

"Largo" page 18.

Make this piece easier to learn and play by doing the following: play the right hand as written, but in the left hand, play only the first note of each measure.

"Kum-Ba-Yah" page 19.

Simplify by playing the right hand as written and only the bass line (bottom note of each chord) in the left hand.

Lap Tap and Play:

"Kum-Ba-Yah" page 19.

Tap the rhythm of the right-hand part on your knee while the left hand plays the chords on the piano.

"Welcome To My World" page 20.

Tap the rhythm of the right-hand part on your knee while the left hand plays its part on the piano. Next, play the right-hand on the piano while you tap the left hand and name the left-hand notes.

4 CHALLENGES

Challenges

Challenges give you the opportunity to check your understanding and test your skill by using what you have learned in new, similar, or altered situations. New learnings can then become the foundation for further progress.

 ## Staff Reading:

Refer to the READ and PLAY melodies on page 52.
- Teach the left hand to play melodies 1 and 2; teach the right hand to play melodies 3 and 4. Read the starting note, intervals, and direction, but not letter names.
- You may also choose to double the melodies by playing them in both hands at the same time, parallel motion.
- Play Melodies 7 and 8 beginning on different pitches and using different five-finger patterns beginning on white keys (F and G). This is called TRANSPOSITION.

Melody 7 transposed to the G five-finger pattern

"**Largo**" PIECES BY CHOICE page 18.

- Teach your left hand to play the melody; play it one octave lower than written.

Play one octave lower than written

- Rewrite the first four measures in 2/4 meter. The piece will look different, but the sound will be the same.

"**Kum-Ba-Yah**" PIECES BY CHOICE page 19.

- To test your pitch awareness, sing, hum, or whistle the melody while you play the left hand as written.
- Play the right hand as written while the left hand plays the chords in half notes.

CHALLENGES 4

Comping:

- Practice the F, G and C chords in each pattern.
- Play the two suggested comping patterns below.

"Love Me Tender" page 7.

- COMP THE CHORDS in one of the two ways above. Sing, or let the Disk/CD/Tape play the melody while you comp the chords.

"Welcome To My World" page 20.

- Read the chord symbols and decide on a comp style appropriate to this tune. Play along with the Disk/CD/Tape or COMP while someone else plays or sings the melody with you.

CHAPTER 5: Key Signatures, Minor Triads, & Inversions

Pieces No Choice

("Major Crossings," "A Minor Waltz," "Fiddler On The Roof," "Climb Ev'ry Mountain,") pages 21, 22, 37, & 38

Pieces By Choice

"Für Elise" page 23.

"Alleluia" page 26.

"806 Rag" page 24.

Key Signatures:

The sharps or flats at the beginning of each staff indicate the key signature.

Sharps and Flats

Sharps or flats in the key signature tell you which notes to play sharped or flatted throughout the piece.

Play
F♯

In The Key Of...

The key signature helps to identify the key in which a composition is written. For example, a piece of music is "in the key of G," when the key signature displays one sharp, when the tonal center (key note) is G, and when the piece uses the tones from the G major scale.

Key Signature of G Major: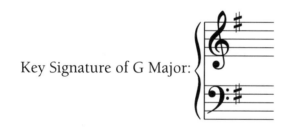

Relative Minor

Every major key has a RELATIVE MINOR key that shares the same key signature.
- The relative minor key note is the 6th tone of the major scale.
- G major's relative minor is E minor, one sharp. C major's relative minor is A minor, no flats or sharps. See KEY SIGNATURES in Appendix A for all other keys and key signatures.

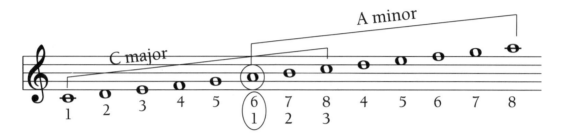

Pieces "In The Key Of..."

Some examples of key signatures follow:

C Major
A Minor

"Für Elise"
"Sun Of My Soul"

F Major
D Minor

"Alleluia"
"The Phantom Of The Opera"

G Major
E Minor

"To A Wild Rose"
"806 Rag"

Minor Triad:

A minor triad is formed from a major triad (1-3-5) by lowering the third a half step (1-♭3-5). The symbol for a minor triad is the alphabet letter followed by a small "m," such as Cm.

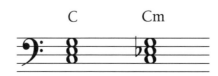

Inversions:

Root position triads are built in thirds on the staff (line-line-line, or space-space-space). The chord members are designated "root," "third," and "fifth." Those three notes may be played in different positions, or INVERSIONS, without changing the name of that triad.

- Inversions are determined by the chord member that is on the bottom (the bass note).
- A root position chord becomes "inverted" when the bottom note is taken to the top, leaving the third in the bass.

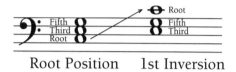

Root Position   1st Inversion

- A 1st inversion triad becomes 2nd inversion when the bottom note is taken to the top, leaving the fifth in the bass.

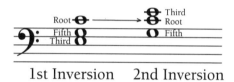

1st Inversion   2nd Inversion

Letter Symbols:

Inversions can be indicated specifically by using letter symbols, such as C/E.

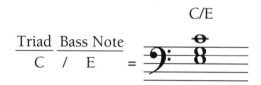

Intervals:
Fourth

A fourth is one step smaller than a fifth. On the staff the notes appear on a line and a space, or on a space and a line.

- Within a five-finger position, a FOURTH can be played between fingers 5 and 2, or between 4 and 1, in either hand.
- To play a FOURTH within your hand position, skip two fingers.

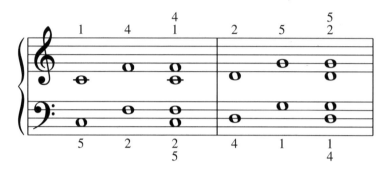

Sixth

A sixth is one step larger than a fifth. On the staff the notes appear on a line and a space, or on a space and a line.

- A sixth is normally played with fingers 1 and 5 in either hand.
- From the five-finger position the hand extends to reach a sixth, with the top note moving up, or the bottom note moving down.

Intervals Within Triads

When playing triads and inversions, notice the intervals and the standard fingerings indicated. Use consistent fingering.

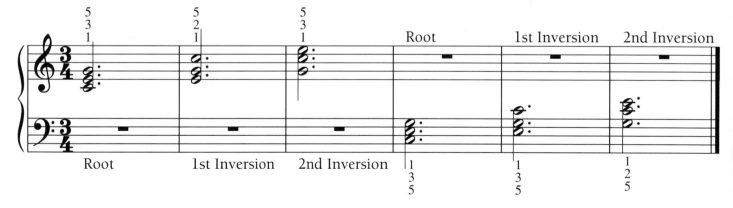

Comparative Interval Reading:

One shortcut to fluent reading and rapid recognition is to compare all intervals to thirds and fifths. Thirds occur on two consecutive lines or two consecutive spaces. Fifths occur on two lines separated by a vacant line, or two spaces separated by a vacant space.

Seconds and Fourths

Compared to a THIRD: a SECOND (line-space, or space-line) is one step smaller, a FOURTH (line-space, or space-line) is one step larger.

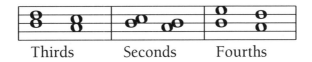

Fourths and Sixths

Compared to fifths: a FOURTH is one step smaller, a SIXTH is one step larger.

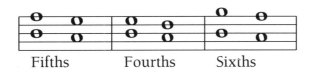

Quick Recognition

Odd-numbered intervals (THIRDS and FIFTHS) always occur on two lines or two spaces. Even-numbered intervals (SECONDS, FOURTHS and SIXTHS) always occur on space-line or line-space combinations. Memorize and recognize these visual distances.

FACTS

Changing Hand Positions:

Few pieces of music can be played by remaining entirely within a single five-finger position. When it is necessary to extend or change positions, use one of the following three possibilities:

Lift and Place your hand in a new five-finger position, following appropriate musical considerations and phrasing.

"Fiddler On The Roof" (PIECES No CHOICE) page 37.

Extend or Contract your hand to move higher or lower in a smooth and connected manner.

"Für Elise," (PIECES BY CHOICE) page 23.

Finger Crossings

Another method for extending the hand position is to cross thumbs under third or fourth finger, or to cross third and fourth finger over thumbs. Sometimes such fingerings are indicated within the music. Notice that fingerings are written above the right-hand part and below the left-hand part.

"A Minor Waltz" measures 1–3 (PIECES No CHOICE) page 22.   "A Minor Waltz" measures 9–11 (PIECES No CHOICE) page 22.

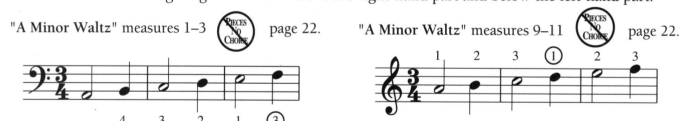

Touch:

Legato

Unless indicated otherwise, piano music is played in a smooth and connected manner. The Italian term for this is LEGATO. Legato playing can be further indicated in the music by phrase marks, or slurs. (See "Kum-Ba-Yah," PIECES BY CHOICE, page 19.) All the notes under one slur are to be played legato

legato, slurred

Staccato

This term directs you to play in a short and detached manner - not connected. Staccato is indicated by a dot over or under a note.

staccato, detached

D.C. and D.S.:

Da Capo al Fine (D.C.)
Repeat from the beginning and play to the word "Fine" (pronounced "fee-nay"), the end.

Dal Segno (D.S.)
Repeat from the sign.

Transposition:

When the same intervals, rhythms, and patterns of notes are written or played in a different key, they are "transposed" from the original key. The melodic excerpt below has been transposed from the key of C, to the keys of F and G.

Key of C   Key of F   Key of G

Accompaniment Styles:

In piano solos the melody often occurs in the treble clef and is played with the right hand while the accompaniment occurs in the bass clef and is played with the left hand. The following accompaniment styles are commonly found in left-hand parts; familiarity with them will provide a shortcut to learning many more pieces.

Block Chord   Broken Chord   Single Line

Division of Note Values:

Normally, a note value divides into two equal parts. ♩ = ♪♪; ♪ = ♬ ; and so on. Composers can choose to change the natural division of a note by indicating that it is to be divided into three parts: ♬♪ – a TRIPLET. The feeling of the quarter-note pulse remains the same. You simply divide the beat into three parts instead of the usual two.

Performance Style:

When eighth notes (♪♪) appear in music, they are sometimes played differently, depending on the style of the piece.

- In classical music eighth notes are played evenly. The same is true for popular and rock music.

- In the blues, or in swing-style popular music, the eighth notes are played unevenly, making them sound "long-short-long-short," such as ♩ ♪ .

Written   Played

Preps

Practice, Read, Play, Remember!

🎵 Tap and Count (L, R, TOG.):

To set the tempo and feel the beat, count two measures before you begin - EVERY TIME! It saves lots of startovers and lowers frustration.

5 PREPS

◎ Finger Taps:

Staff Reading:

The following brief examples are for daily reading and transposition. Read by interval (direction and distance) and pattern. Use the READING GUIDES. Remember that you are practicing how to read comparatively. Look for THIRDS and FIFTHS; compare them to SECONDS, FOURTHS, and SIXTHS. Notice the key signature before playing. Follow this plan:

- Check KEY SIGNATURE, METER, and CLEFS.
- Practice FINGER TAPS and COUNT.
- Practice FINGER TAPS and say LETTER NAMES.
- PLAY: keep eyes on music.
- Refer to FACTS: TRANSPOSITION on page 67 and transpose the following examples to C, F, or G.

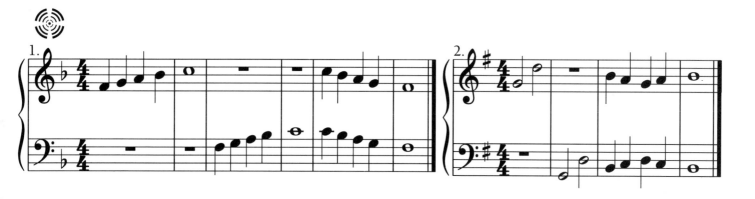

5 PREPS

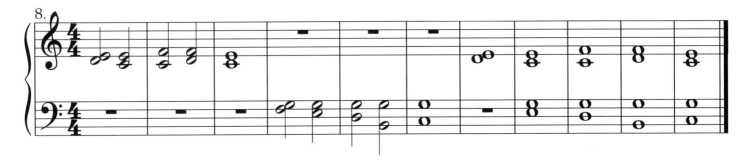

◉ Finger Crossings:

Practice finger crossings by playing the following. Play "Major Crossings" (C major scale), PIECES NO CHOICE, page 21, and "A Minor Waltz" (A minor scale), PIECES NO CHOICE, page 22, to experience two traditional scale fingerings. Watch for similar "crossing" opportunities within PIECES BY CHOICE and all other music.

◉ Altered Hand Positions:

The succession of notes on the staff may require alterations within the original five-finger starting position, as in the following.

- Place your right hand in the Middle C position. Close your eyes and with your third finger, feel for E♭. When you change your third finger to E♭, the pattern becomes C minor. (Return to C major.)
- While in the C position, move your right-hand fourth finger to F♯, thus making the pattern C-D-E-F♯-G. Are your eyes still closed? (Return to C major position.)
- Using the left hand, repeat the two steps above making appropriate adjustments in fingerings. Keep your eyes closed.
- Refer to the PIECES BY CHOICE section and play "Climb Ev'ry Mountain" on page 38, first with the right hand, then the left hand. The melody stays within a five-note range, but sometimes E and F are altered. Make those changes without looking at your hands.

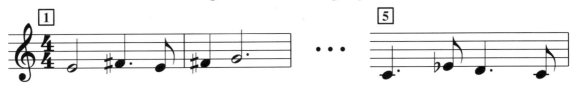

⟫ Arpeggios:

Hand positions can be extended by lifting and placing the hand in a new position. In this example an arpeggio simply extends the broken chord played in the left hand (5-3-1), then in the right hand (1-3-5).

Hand-Over-Hand

Cross the left hand over the right hand and repeat each pattern one octave higher, making a total of four broken chords, L R L R, as in the example below.

Broken-Chord Patterns

Play arpeggios on the following four-measure "sets" of chords, referring to the SCALE CHART on page 104 of the Appendix.

• C F G C

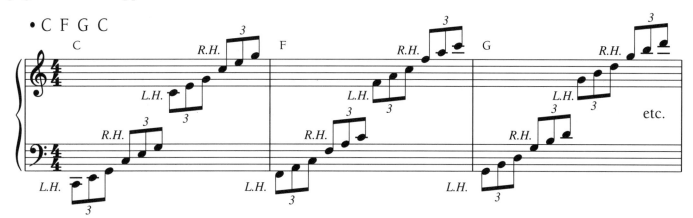

• G C D G
• F B♭ C F
• Dm Gm A Dm

Hints

Always use 5-3-1 in left hand, 1-3-5 in right hand.
Memorize the black key/white key combinations of each chord shape.
How is your "bilateral" coordination?

Reps

Practice every day. The length of time is less important than the regularity. Organize practice so that you improve skills specifically, rather than simply "going over the pieces." Take a few minutes at every practice time to: warm up, tap and read, and study a section of one or two specific pieces. Then, spend the rest of the time (as much as you want) on your CHOICE of materials.

Warm-ups:

Be sure to play several warm-ups each time you start to practice. Use melodies from STAFF READING in the PREPS section of any chapter.
- Play as written and transpose to the C, F, or G five-finger patterns.
- Read and verbalize away from the piano by saying letter names, intervals and direction.

"Alleluia" page 26.
- Play the left hand as written while you tap and chant the finger numbers of the right hand.
- Play the right hand as written while you tap the rhythm of the left hand on your left knee.
- Play the left hand as written. In measures 1-8, block the interval in each measure of the left hand.
- Name each interval as you block and play each measure of the left hand.

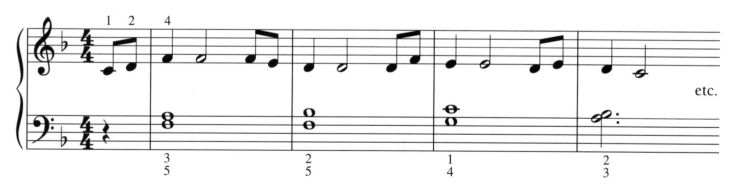

ꗞ Shortcuts:

"Für Elise" page 23.

- PLAY and COUNT: Play the right hand as written while blocking the left hand.

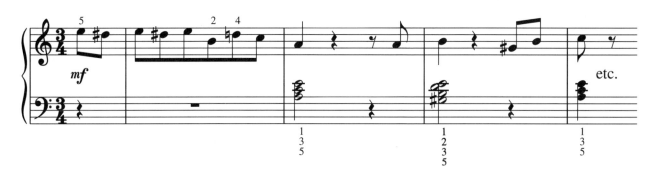

- PLAY the following blocked sequence from measures 10-13.

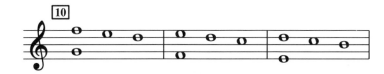

- OBSERVE the slurs in measures 2, 3, 6, and 7. They connect some left-hand notes with right-hand notes. Make smooth connections and shape the melodic phrases between hands.

5 CHALLENGES

Challenges

Listening:

Listen to recordings of Scott Joplin's ragtime music or Beethoven's "Für Elise" to further acquaint yourself with the style of this music. Recordings will be easy to find in a library, record store, or in a friend's collection.

Rhythm Track for "806 Rag:" page 24.

Assemble a collection of real or "improvised" rhythm instruments. Experiment with a variety of sounds and patterns that sound fun. Record a rhythmic accompaniment tape to play with "806 Rag." Can you notate the rhythmic parts you have played?

Comping "Climb Ev'ry Mountain:" page 38.

Review the comping of "Love Me Tender" on page 59 of Chapter 4.

- Study the chord symbols above the lead line of "Climb Ev'ry Mountain," and simplify each chord to its basic triad. For example, D7 = D; Gmaj7 = G; Gm7 = Gm; C7 = C; and so on.

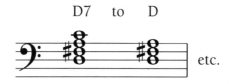

- Sing, or let the Disk/CD/Tape play the melody while you comp the chords.

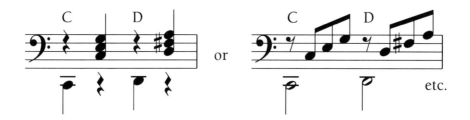

Comping "Fiddler On The Roof:" page 37.

Note: pickup notes (incomplete measures) are not usually chorded. Begin comping where the chord symbol begins.

• Use the following BASS/CHORD rhythm patterns as two possibilities.

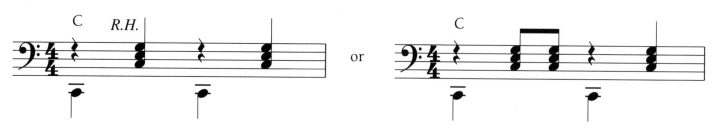

or

• Practice moving back and forth between the C chord and the D♭ chord without looking at your hands. The distance is only a half step. Try not to lift your hands too far off the keys while playing or shifting from one chord to the next. Play with relaxed arms and wrists, moving smoothly between the two chords.

CHAPTER 6 : Common-Tone Voicing & Dominant Sevenths

Pieces No Choice
("Help Me Make It Through The Night," "You Needed Me") pages 38 & 39.

Pieces By Choice

"Swan Lake Theme"  page 27.

"Michael, Row The Boat Ashore" page 28.

Common-Tone Voicing:

When two triads share one or two of the same chord members, they have notes in common, or "common tones." For example, the C triad (C-E-G) and the G triad (G-B-D) each contain G, a common tone. The F triad (F-A-C) and the Dm triad (D-F-A) have two tones in common, F and A.

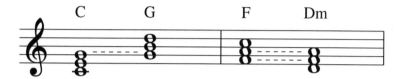

- Why should you care about common-tone voicing? You have probably discovered that when all chords are played in root position, they jump around a lot. In addition to being more difficult to play, an inferior musical sound often results. By using inversions of some triads, the chords sound smoother and become easier to connect.

- In moving from one chord to another, COMMON-TONE VOICING retains the common tone in the same voice (bottom, middle, or top). The other members of the chord are "inverted" to accomodate the position of the common tone.

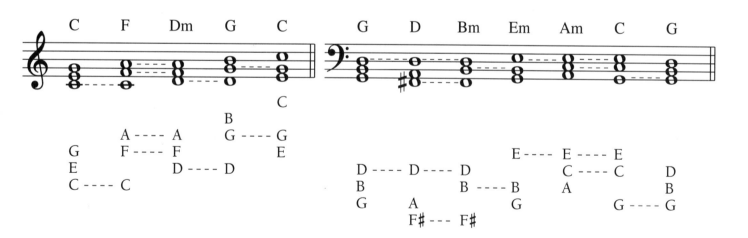

Intervals:

Octave

An OCTAVE is the interval of an "eighth." The musical alphabet has seven different letters,
A B C D E F G. If we continue one more letter, the alphabet starts over with another A. The
first A and second A become an OCTAVE apart, eight letter names.

- Octaves are normally played with fingers 1 and 5 and can occur between any two letter names that
  are the same, C and C, B♭ and B♭, F and F, and so on.
- On the staff, octaves appear on a line and a space, or on a space and a line, widely separated.

Seventh

The interval of a SEVENTH is one letter name smaller than an octave. On the staff, sevenths appear
on two lines or two spaces, widely separated. Sevenths are played between fingers 1 and 4, or 1 and 5
in either hand.

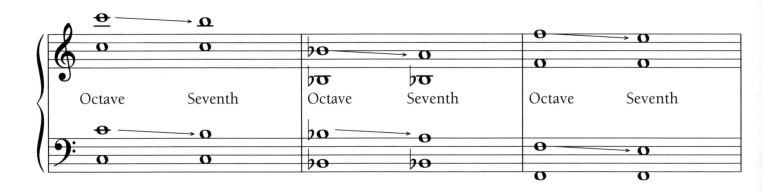

- In addition to the alphabetical measurement, sevenths can be further defined by a "quality" name.
  Major sevenths and minor sevenths are two common quality designations.
- A major seventh interval is the distance from the first to the seventh degree of a major scale, or one
  half step smaller than an octave. A minor seventh interval is two half steps smaller than an octave.

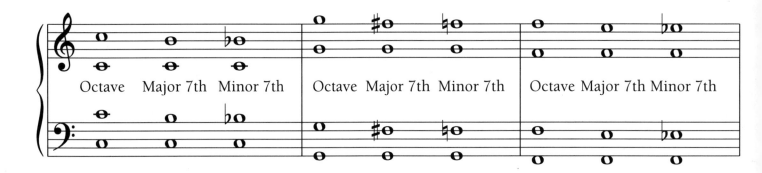

Seventh Chords:

Seventh chords are made up of four notes, root-third-fifth-seventh. (Remember that triads are three-note chords made up of root-third-fifth.) To find the notes of any chord, use the major scale built on the root of that chord.

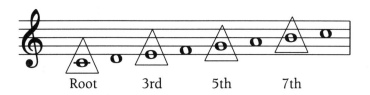

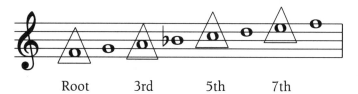

The most common of all seventh chords is the DOMINANT SEVENTH.

- The chord symbol used for dominant 7th chords is made up of the alphabet letter (root of chord) and the number "7." For example, C7, B♭7, G7, and F7 are all symbols for dominant 7ths.

- To build a dominant 7th chord, start with the major triad. Add a minor seventh (two half steps smaller than an octave).

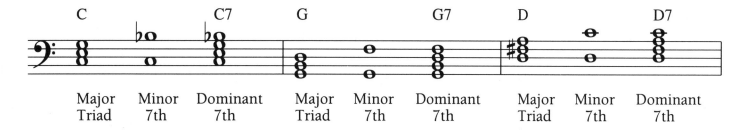

- When using 7th chords in common-tone voicings, the fifth of the chord is often left out to maintain three voices, as in a triad. The following examples show dominant 7th chords and their inversions, minus the fifth of the chord.

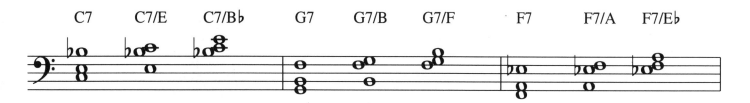

 # Facts

Circle of Keys (Major):

The CIRCLE OF MAJOR KEYS illustrates the logical order and relationships of scales, chords, and key signatures.

- If you think of moving from left to right on the piano, the CIRCLE OF KEYS progresses clockwise in fifths; counterclockwise in fourths.

- Three pairs of ENHARMONIC keys occur at the bottom of the circle: D♭-C♯, G♭-F♯, and C♭-B. Two keys are enharmonic when they have the same sound, but different names. For example, D♭ and C♯ have the same sound.

- The CIRCLE OF KEYS will be a valuable guide in organizing your practice. You do not need to memorize it or fully understand it at this time. You will be referring back to it many times during upcoming lessons and will master it a little at a time.

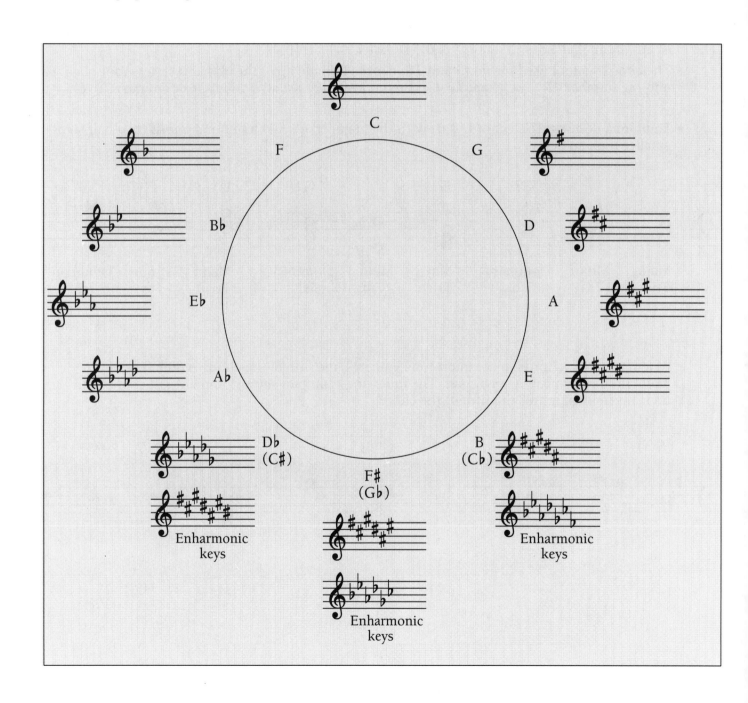

Preps

Perceive, Practice, and Perfect patterns in music. At each practice session, focus primarily on one or two tasks that you can improve forever. Master these improvements and build on them. Review older skills and retain them.

Tap and Count (L, R, TOG.):

Count two measures in tempo before you begin to tap. Tap and count as you feel a continous beat. "The beat goes on" whether you do or not! Remember, use your right hand to tap the notes with stems up and your left hand for those with the stems down.

Tap and Play:

Time to get coordinated! Before playing patterns 1 and 2 on the keyboard, tap the appropriate fingers in rhythm (L, R, TOG). On the piano, continue the patterns throughout one octave.

Variations on Patterns 1 and 2

• Play patterns 1 and 2 again, but this time, play each five-finger pattern descending.

• Alternate the direction of the five-finger patterns in the hand playing eighth notes. Play the first measure ascending, second measure descending, third measure ascending, and so on as your hand positions continue to progress upward.

• Create different rhythm patterns for greater variety.

Staff Reading:

Turn to page 38 in the PIECES BY CHOICE pull-out section and read "Help Me Make It Through the Night" and "You Needed Me." Play each melody first with the right hand alone and then with the left hand alone (one octave lower than written). It will help to practice in these ways:

- Tap the rhythm and count.
- Verbalize the direction and distance of the intervals. For example, "Help Me Make It Through the Night" begins "G, up a third, up, down, down, up, down a sixth," and so on.
- Tap the rhythm and say the letter names of the notes.
- Focus on the newest intervals we have learned to read - 6th, 7th and octave. They are all outside of a five-finger position.

Chords and Inversions:

- Spell the following chords - G C Am D7 G. (Do not include the 5th in D7.)
- Play the chords in the right hand only.

All root position, root on bottom, fingering 1-3-5.
(Use 1-2-5 for D7.)

All first inversion, root on top, fingering 1-2-5.
(Use 1-4-5 for D7.)

All second inversion, root in the middle, fingering 1-3-5.
(Use 1-2-4 for D7.)

- Play the chords as above, using left hand only, fingering as follows:

5-3-1

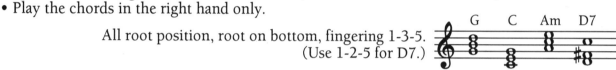

5-3-1 (Use 5-2-1 for D7.)

5-2-1 (Use 4-3-1 for D7.)

Chord Progression Using Common-Tone Voicing:

- Now, play the following progression using common-tone voicing. Identify the common tones and the inversions used to achieve these smooth connections.

PREPS

Building Dominant Sevenths:

Use the following example to practice building dominant 7th chords around the circle of keys, counter-clockwise. Moving in this direction produces the cycle of fourths.

- Start at various places on the circle and learn two or three chords each practice session until you have completed the entire circle.
- When you master the chords in the right hand, teach your left hand to play the dominant sevenths. Use fingering, 5 3 2 1.

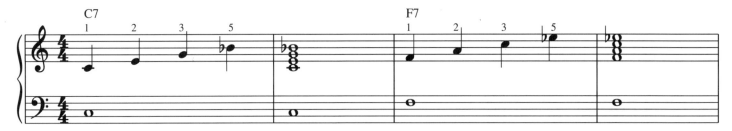

Accompaniment Styles:

A shortcut to learning and reading a new piece of music is to recognize the chords and patterns in the accompaniment. You have already learned three common styles: broken-chord, block-chord, and single-line.

"Swan Lake Theme" (Pieces By Choice) page 27.

Example 1 below is an excerpt of the left-hand part. Notice that when the broken chord accompaniment is blocked in Example 2, it clearly shows that common-tone voicing is being used throughout the piece. This will simplify the coordination of the left hand and will be of great value in learning the piece securely. Practice with blocked and broken chords.

"Michael, Row The Boat Ashore" (Pieces By Choice) page 28.

This piece uses fifths, sixths, and sevenths in a modified block-chord accompaniment style simplified to two voices. Practice the following two PREPS to help you get the feel of these most recently learned intervals, sixths and sevenths, in the key of G major.

- Practice both sets of fingering indicated. Play them both in a smooth and connected manner.

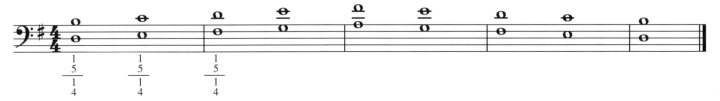

- Play the following PREP by sliding the thumb down a second in each measure while holding the bottom note. Each measure changes from the interval of a 7th, to a 6th.

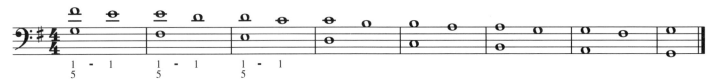

Reps

This section of the chapter helps guide you to practice in the most efficient ways. These suggestions present shortcuts to mastery of the skills you need to play the piano well. They strengthen what you already know, making it second-nature to play. Really!

"Für Elise" page 23.

Using what you have learned in this chapter, find and play the common tones between the two chord patterns in measures 1 and 2. Do likewise for measures 10 and 11; 12 and 13.

Name the chord and its inversion in measure 2. If you name and recognize these chord shapes, you will no longer have to "read" them in detail. Your hand will remember the chord shape and play it.

"806 Rag" page 24.

Spell the D7 (dominant 7th) chord. Spell it again, omitting the 5th. Play this chord. Turn to the "806 Rag" and circle all the D7 chords in that piece.

"Somewhere Out There" page 29.

Locate instances of common tones between chords in the left hand and draw a line connecting them. Also locate and play all D7, Fmaj7, and G7/F chords.

REPS

Arpeggios:

Play hand-over-hand arpeggios on the following new set of chords, D E A D.
Review the C F G C set, also.

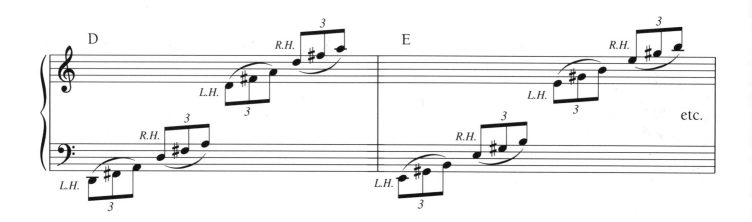

Triad and Inversion Scales:

Using only the tones of the C major scale, play each of the following block-chord positions throughout the C scale, ascending and descending, using correct fingering. You may also play them using broken chords. This skill will reward you generously if you develop it now. (This is sort of like "eating your spinach." Some people like it, some hate it, but it's good for everybody!)

Play the following examples one octave higher than written.

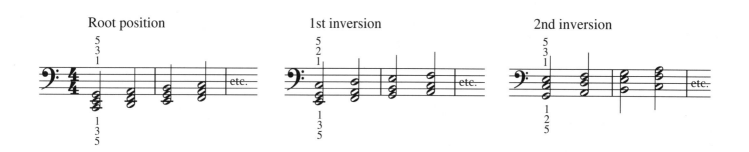

Challenges

Circle of Keys:

Review the CIRCLE OF KEYS found in FACTS 6 page 82.

- Play the key-notes as you move clockwise from key to key on the circle and from left to right on the piano. This creates the CIRCLE OF FIFTHS.

- Do not change direction, assuming your piano has 88 keys. If not, adjust. Beginning with the lowest C on your piano, play two notes in each hand, using fingers 5 1 in the left hand and 1 5 in the right hand. Play hand over hand: LH = C G; RH = D A; LH = E B; and so on. If you put the damper pedal down and keep it down throughout the cycle, you will hear a sound similar to the sound check that precedes many CD and taped recordings.

(Play two octaves lower than written.)

- Can you play the CIRCLE OF FIFTHS counterclockwise using left-hand fingering 5 2 and right-hand fingering 2 5?

"Michael, Row The Boat Ashore" page 28.

Using only the G, C, and D (or D7) chords, play a more traditional block-chord accompaniment to the melody. Use your ear to help you discover the correct chords. Go ahead and use Em in one place, if you feel you want to.

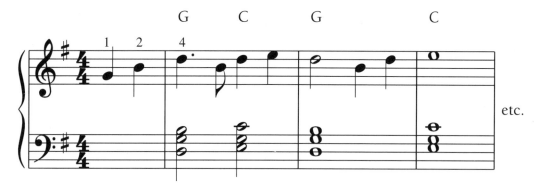

6 CHALLENGES

"Swan Lake Theme" page 27.

Play the melody with the left hand two octaves lower than written. Block the chords in the right hand and play them above middle C. It may require some experimentation to find the "right" chords for measures 3 and 7.

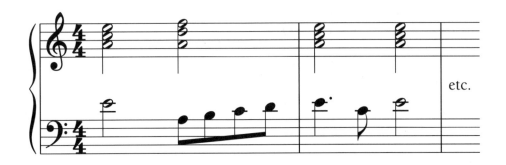

"Climb Ev'ry Mountain" page 38.

Create a majestic chordal accompaniment with both hands. You will only be playing chords on the piano, so sing, record, or imagine the melody. Read and play from the chord symbols, but do not write out the accompaniment.

- Reduce every chord symbol to its basic triad: C=C, D7=D, Gmaj7=G, Fmaj7=F, Fm6=Fm, and so on.
- As indicated above the staff, chords last either two counts, or four counts. Adapt the accompaniment appropriately and play as in the following excerpt, slowly and majestically. These are the Alps, you know!
- After you have practiced in this way for a while, you may wish to try some inversions on the chords that last four beats.

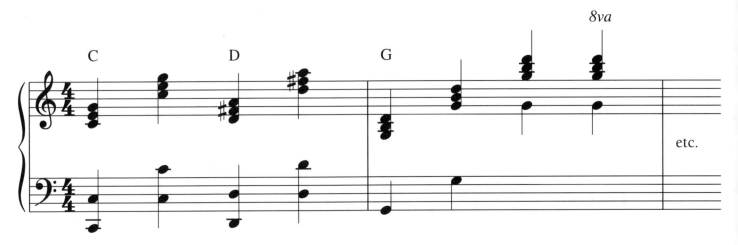

CHAPTER 7 : Augmented & Diminished Triads, Sus & Sixth Chords

Pieces No Choice
("Joshua Fought The Battle Of Jericho," "Deep River," "Melody In F")   page 40.

Pieces By Choice

"To A Wild Rose" page 36.

"Softly And Tenderly" page 32.

Facts
(Major and Minor Triads, Augmented Triad, Diminished Triad, Sus, 6th Chords, Syncopation, Chromatic Movement, 8va, 15va, loco)

Preps
(Tap and Count, Tap and Play, MAmd, Staff Reading, Observe, New Scales, Arpeggios, Accompaniment Patterns)

Reps
(Warm-ups, "To A Wild Rose," "Softly And Tenderly," "The Phantom Of The Opera")

Challenges
(Improvise, Harmonize - "Deep River," "Melody in F")

FACTS

Major and Minor Triads:

Remember that major triads are built using the first, third and fifth tones of a major scale (1-3-5). (See Major Scales Chart in Appendix B on page 104.) A minor triad is formed from a major triad by lowering the third a half step (1-♭3-5).

Augmented Triad:

An AUGMENTED TRIAD is formed from a major triad by raising the fifth a half step (1-3-♯5). The symbol for an augmented triad is the alphabet letter followed by + or +5, such as C+, or C+5.

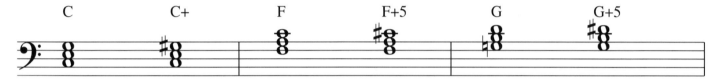

Diminished Triad:

A DIMINISHED TRIAD is formed from a minor triad (1-♭3-5) by lowering the fifth a half step (1-♭3-♭5). It can also be formed from a major triad by lowering two tones: the third and the fifth. The symbol for a diminished triad is the alphabet letter followed by "dim," such as Cdim. Also, C° is sometimes used.

Sus:

SUS is used in lead lines and chord symbols as an abbreviation for "suspension." When "sus" follows a chord symbol, it indicates that the third of the chord should be left out and that the fourth degree of the scale should be played in its place. Although symbols such as "Gsus" are limited to popular music and lead lines in fake books, the "sound" of a sus chord is found in music of all styles.

6th Chords:

A 6th CHORD is created by adding the sixth degree of the scale to a major or minor triad. For example, F and Fm refer to the F major and F minor triads. F6 and Fm6 refer to the addition of the sixth scale degree to each chord. The added sixth is a whole step above the fifth of the chord.

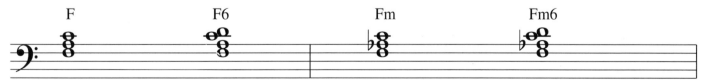

Syncopation:

The beat in music is sometimes referred to as "pulse," because it is regular, steady, and continuous. Meters organize the beats in a measure into patterns of normally stressed beats. A rhythm pattern is SYNCOPATED when stress is placed on a normally unstressed beat or portion of a beat.

- In normal patterns in $\frac{4}{4}$ meter the natural stress is on counts 1 and 3.

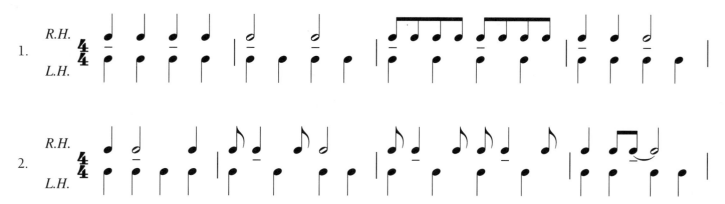

- Although syncopation appears in all styles of music, it is especially important to popular music and jazz. Particularly in popular idioms, syncopated notes need to receive some additional emphasis, even beyond that which happens within the notation.

- To decipher syncopated rhythms, focus on two constants: the "feel" of the underlying pulse, and the note value that represents the continuous division of the beat (in most cases, the eighth note.) To be comfortable with syncopated rhythms, feel the beat in quarter notes, read and count eighth notes, and play any combination, simultaneously.

Chromatic Movement:

When notes move by half step, they move CHROMATICALLY. Downward chromatic movement is notated with flats; upward chromatic movement is notated with sharps.

"The Phantom of the Opera" measures 1-4

8va, 15ma, and loco:

- **8va** is a musical shorthand for octave. When 8va is placed above or below the staff it means to play one octave higher or lower than written. See the above musical example from "The Phantom of the Opera."
- **15ma** is musical shorthand for two octaves. (That's correct; count the keys!) 15ma means to play two octaves higher, or lower, than written.
- **LOCO** is an Italian word meaning to play at the written pitch. "Loco" appears when 8va, or 15ma are cancelled.

8va _ _ _ _ _ _ _ _ _ _ _ _ _ _ _ _ _ _   *15ma* _ _ _ _ _ _ _ _ _ _ _ _ _ _ _ _ _ _   *loco*

7 PREPS
Preps

Practice your understanding of the new FACTS by using them in the following activities. You will also be preparing to learn the PIECES BY CHOICE that require these same musical skills.

Tap and Count:

Tap and Play:

Can you rub your stomach and pat your head at the same time? Change hands and do it again. It takes coordination! Before playing the two patterns below on the keyboard, tap the appropriate fingers in rhythm (L, R, TOG). When you play them on the piano, continue the patterns throughout one octave, ascending and descending.

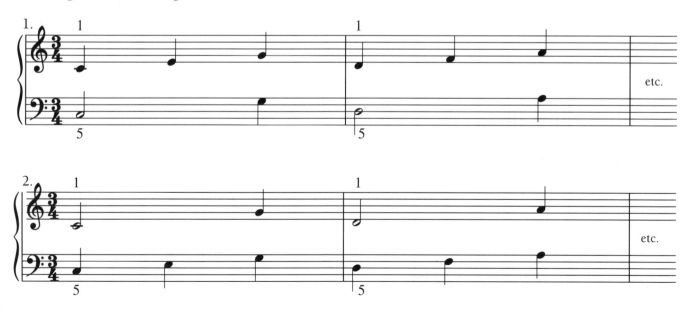

♪ MAmd:

Practice forming the four basic triads: Major, Augmented, minor, and diminished in all keys; play each hand separately. By playing them in the following order you will make two observations:

- It is only necessary to move one voice, one half step at a time, to progress downward through all triads and keys. Always use 5 3 1 in the left hand and 1 3 5 in the right hand.
- The alphabet letter name of the chord (the root) remains the same for a set of Major, Augmented, Major, minor, diminished triads. The letter names (spelling) of the triad members remain the same, even though the flats and sharps alter the chords from major to minor, and so on.

Staff Reading:
STOP!!

Turn to page 40 in the PIECES BY CHOICE pull-out section and read "Joshua Fought The Battle Of Jericho," "Deep River," and "Melody In F."

Before you try to play these melodies, read them away from the keyboard. Verbalize in rhythm: first, direction and distance; then, letter names. Next, play the melody with one hand, then the other.

♪ Observe:

- As you were playing the previous three melodies, how many of the following FACTS from this chapter did you find? Read the following, then return to the melodies and play them again. Perhaps you can also play the chords or just a bass line.

"Joshua Fought The Battle Of Jericho" page 40.
SYNCOPATION in every measure, except 1, 5, and 8.

"Deep River" page 40.
Eb AUGMENTED CHORD in measures 1 and 5.

"Melody in F" page 40.
Two DIMINISHED TRIADS.

- The following lead line excerpt is the dramatic ending of the complete, "Climb Ev'ry Mountain." Notice how the chords increase the feeling of tension and drama in the third and fourth measures from the end. Play those chords and remember the sound.

⁊PREPS

New Scales:

When preparing to play a piece of music, one of the best ways to orient yourself is to play the scale. In Chapter 5 you played the C major scale (the key of "Climb Ev'ry Mountain") and the A minor scale (the key of "Für Elise"). Now you will learn the scales of the PIECES BY CHOICE in this chapter.

"To A Wild Rose" G MAJOR, one ♯. page 36.

- Play up and down the scale from G to G, using the same fingering as the C scale (being sure to include F♯ from the key signature.)

R.H. 1 2 3 1 2 3 4 5

L.H. 5 4 3 2 1 3 2 1

"Softly And Tenderly" F MAJOR, one ♭. page 32.

- Play up and down the scale from F to F, using the same fingering as the C and G scales in the left hand only. In the right hand, use 1 2 3 4, 1 2 3 4, which allows you to cross after the fourth finger on the B♭.

Same fingering as C major scale   *R.H.* 1 2 3 4 1 2 3 4

L.H. 5 4 3 2 1 3 2 1

"The Phantom Of The Opera" D MINOR, one ♭. page 34.

- Play up and down the scale from D to D, using the same fingering as the A minor scale (being sure to include the B♭ from the key signature.)
- Refer to "A Minor Waltz," in the PIECES BY CHOICE section, page 23.
- A complete descending D minor scale occurs in the melody of this piece. Find it and practice the scale fingering there.

R.H. 1 2 3 1 2 3 4 5

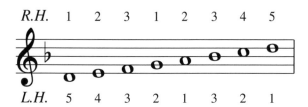

L.H. 5 4 3 2 1 3 2 1

◉ Arpeggios:

Refer to the PREPS section of Chapter 5 page 73. Play hand-over-hand arpeggios on the following new sets of chords. These harmonies will be found in the PIECES BY CHOICE in this chapter.

- G   Gsus   D   G
- F   F+5   B♭   F
- Dm   Gm   C♯dim   Dm

Accompaniment Patterns:

Practice the following three accompaniment patterns from the PIECES BY CHOICE. It is essential that you memorize the "look" and the "feel" of these patterns so that you can play them comfortably. Notice the many instances of common-tone voicing.

"To A Wild Rose" 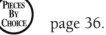 page 36.

Also practice this accompaniment one octave higher than written.

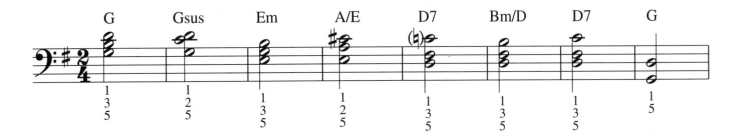

"Softly And Tenderly" page 32.

Retain the image of blocked chords while playing the broken-chord accompaniment.

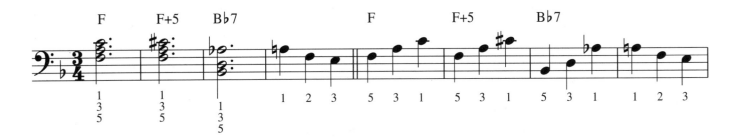

"The Phantom Of The Opera" page 34.

Also learn this accompaniment substituting the C#dim chord for C major. Both occur in the arrangement.

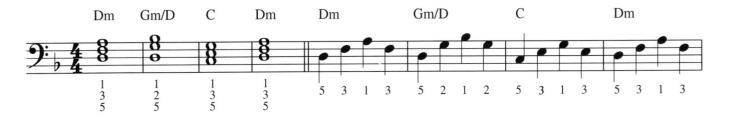

7 REPS
Reps

When practicing the piano, keep two consistent goals in mind: hold on to what you've got and reach out for more! Review the old skills and information while you learn the new.

Warm-ups:

- Turn to the PREPS section in Chapter 6 and review TAP and PLAY.
  Play the patterns moving up CHROMATICALLY (C, C♯, D, D♯, etc), using all major triads.
  Play the patterns throughout one octave of the G major and the F major scales.

- Play hand-over-hand arpeggios on this set of triads - D♭ E♭ A♭ D♭.

- Play the following chords to practice building and resolving dominant 7th chords. Notice that the notated sample is a section of the CIRCLE OF KEYS, page 82. Play chords built on E, A, and D in a similar manner, using another section of the circle.

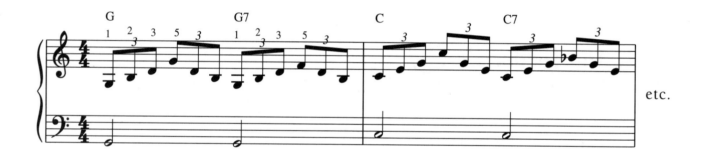

"To A Wild Rose" (Pieces By Choice) page 36.

After identifying all of the chords in the accompaniment and playing them in the left hand, practice in these two additional ways:

- Play the right hand as written and play only the bass note of each left hand chord.

- Play the left hand as written and play only the first note of each measure in the right hand.

etc.

"Softly And Tenderly" page 32.

Practice in four-measure segments - NOT always from the beginning.

- Tap and Count - L, R, TOG.
- Take special note of the syncopation in measures 14, 22, 29, and 30. Know how it feels and what to count.

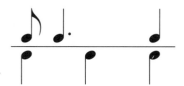

- Practice each hand separately, naming the intervals.
- Play one hand on the keyboard while you tap the rhythm of the other on your knee. Switch hands and repeat. (This practice step is to improve your coordination. Just do it!)
- You may choose to end this piece at measure 16 if you don't want to learn the whole thing.

"The Phantom Of The Opera" page 34.

Follow the same steps as outlined above (with the exception of the last suggestion).

7 CHALLENGES

Challenges

It's time for your final challenges!

Improvise on "To A Wild Rose" page 36.

In the left hand, play the accompaniment for "To A Wild Rose," as written. Create a new right-hand melody. Here are a few suggestions to get you started.

- Use the same pitches in each measure of the original right hand but change the order and the rhythm.

- Make up your own rhythm for a new right hand part, but play the pitches of the original right hand in reverse order.

- Change the meter and/or the accompaniment style.

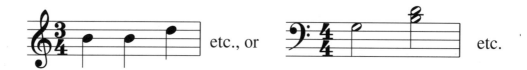

- Write the chord symbols above the right-hand part on the original. Use the tones of each chord as the basis for a new, free-style melody.

Harmonize "Melody In F" (PIECES BY CHOICE) page 40.

Play the chords in the right hand, near or above middle C. (Temporarily leave out the Bdim chord in measure 7.)

- Play the chords in half notes, one per measure.

- Play the chords in quarter notes and count, "1 & 2 &," as you play on the beats.

- Are you ready for a coordination challenge? Continue to play the left hand as written, counting, "1 & 2 &." Now, change the rhythm of the right-hand chords by playing them on the "&'s" instead of on the numbers (the beats). This places the chords on the "off-beats." (You can put Bdim back into measure seven now, because it occurs on the "&" of count 2.)

- For a final challenge, play the melody with the right hand, chords in the left hand.

APPENDIX A - Key Signatures

Major and minor keys that share the same key signature are called relative keys.

MAJOR	KEY SIGNATURE	RELATIVE MINOR
C major	No sharps or flats	a minor
G major	F♯	e minor
D major	F♯, C♯	b minor
A major	F♯, C♯, G♯	f♯ minor
E major	F♯, C♯, G♯, D♯	c♯ minor
B major	F♯, C♯, G♯, D♯, A♯	g♯ minor
F♯ major	F♯, C♯, G♯, D♯, A♯, E♯	d♯ minor
C♯ major	F♯, C♯, G♯, D♯, A♯, E♯, B♯	a♯ minor
F major	B♭	d minor
B♭ major	B♭, E♭	g minor
E♭ major	B♭, E♭, A♭	c minor
A♭ major	B♭, E♭, A♭, D♭	f minor
D♭ major	B♭, E♭, A♭, D♭, G♭	b♭ minor
G♭ major	B♭, E♭, A♭, D♭, G♭, C♭	e♭ minor
C♭ major	B♭, E♭, A♭, D♭, G♭, C♭, F♭	a♭ minor

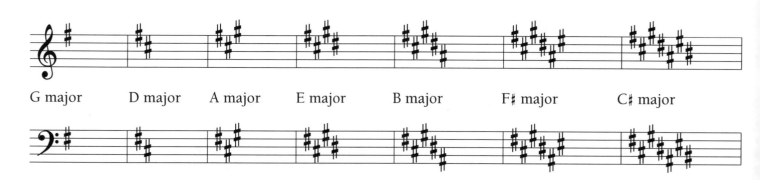

Key signatures of the sharp keys in treble and bass clef.

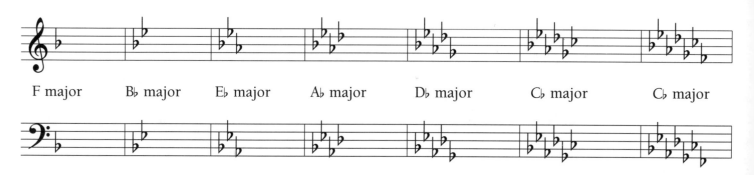

Key signatures of the flat keys in treble and bass clef.

APPENDIX B - Major & Minor Patterns & Scales

Major Five-Finger Patterns

MAJOR FIVE-FINGER PATTERNS: Major five-finger patterns shown below are formed by using the following sequence of whole and half steps. Major five-finger patterns are the first five notes of a major scale and are played with 1, 2, 3, 4, 5 in the right hand; 5, 4, 3, 2, 1 in the left hand.

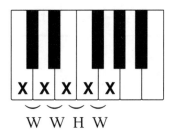

W W H W

MAJOR CHORDS: Major chords are constructed by playing the first, third and fifth degrees of major scales, tones 1, 3 and 5.

MAJOR FIVE-FINGER PATTERNS IN ALL KEYS:

(Sharp Keys)

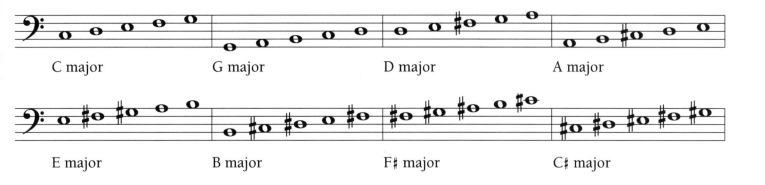

C major   G major   D major   A major

E major   B major   F♯ major   C♯ major

(Flat Keys)

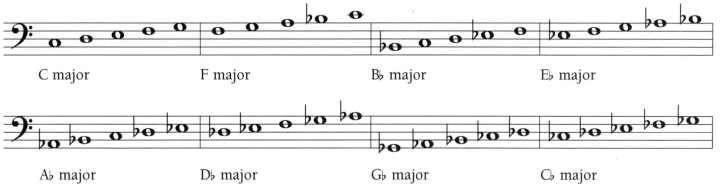

C major   F major   B♭ major   E♭ major

A♭ major   D♭ major   G♭ major   C♭ major

103

Major Scales

TONE 1 Scale Name	TONE 2 (9)	TONE 3	TONE 4 (11)	TONE 5	TONE 6 (13)	TONE 7	TONE 8
C	D	E	F	G	A	B	C
C♯	D♯	E♯(F)	F♯	G♯	A♯	B♯(C)	C♯
D♭	E♭	F	G♭	A♭	B♭	C	D♭
D	E	F♯	G	A	B	C♯	D
E♭	F	G	A♭	B♭	C	D	E♭
E	F♯	G♯	A	B	C♯	D♯	E
F	G	A	B♭	C	D	E	F

TONE 1 Scale Name	TONE 2 (9)	TONE 3	TONE 4 (11)	TONE 5	TONE 6 (13)	TONE 7	TONE 8
F♯	G♯	A♯	B	C♯	D♯	E♯(F)	F♯
G♭	A♭	B♭	C♭(B)	D♭	E♭	F	G♭
G	A	B	C	D	E	F♯	G
A♭	B♭	C	D♭	E♭	F	G	A♭
A	B	C♯	D	E	F♯	G♯	A
B♭	C	D	E♭	F	G	A	B♭
B	C♯	D♯	E	F♯	G♯	A♯	B

Major and Minor Scales:

MAJOR SCALE: A major scale has eight tones and is made up of whole and half steps that occur in the following order:

MINOR SCALE: Each major scale has a RELATIVE MINOR SCALE with the same key signature. The sixth degree of the major scale is the first degree of the RELATIVE MINOR SCALE.

C major

A minor

Three Forms of the Minor Scale

The following three forms of the minor scale are often used.

NATURAL MINOR: (or pure minor) The natural minor scale has the same key signature as the relative major scale.

Natural minor

HARMONIC MINOR: The harmonic scale has the same key signature as the relative minor scale; however, an accidental is used to raise the seventh degree a half step.

Harmonic minor

MELODIC MINOR: The melodic minor scale has the same key signature as the relative major scale; however, accidentals are used to raise the sixth and seventh scale degrees a half step in the ascending scale and to lower them a half step in the descending scale. The melodic minor scale descends the same as the natural minor.

Melodic minor

Minor Five-Finger Patterns

MINOR FIVE-FINGER PATTERNS: Minor five-finger patterns are formed by lowering the middle note of a major five-finger pattern a half step. Minor five-finger patterns are the first five tones of a minor scale.

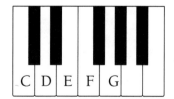

Major Five Finger Pattern

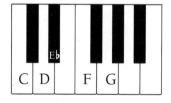

Minor Five Finger Pattern

MINOR CHORDS: Minor chords are constructed by playing the first, third and fifth degrees of minor scales, tones 1, 3 and 5; or, by playing a major chord and lowering the third a half step.

APPENDIX C - Chords
Chord Formulas

The following formulas indicate chord spellings. Each formula refers to the major scale of the chord name. Remember that the tones will not necessarily occur in the music in the same order that is given in the spelling.

TYPE OF CHORD	CHORD SYMBOL	Formula	NOTES (C scale)
MAJOR	C	1-3-5	C-E-G
MINOR	Cm	1-3♭-5	C-E♭-G
DIMINISHED	Cdim (C°)	1-3♭-5♭	C-E♭-G♭
AUGMENTED	C+ (C Aug)	1-3-5♯	C-E-G♯
MAJOR 6th	C6	1-3-5-6	C-E-G-A
MINOR 6th	Cm6	1-3♭-5-6	C-E♭-G-A
DOMINANT 7th	C7	1-3-5-7♭	C-E-G-B♭
MAJOR 7th	Cmaj7	1-3-5-7	C-E-G-B
MINOR 7th	Cm7	1-3♭-5-7♭	C-E♭-G-B♭
MINOR 7 FLAT 5	Cm7-5 (Cm7♭5)	1-3♭-5♭-7♭	C-E♭-G♭-B♭
DIMINISHED 7th	Cdim7	1-3♭-5♭-7♭♭(6)	C-E♭-G♭-B♭♭(A)
DOMINANT NINTH	C9	1-3-5-7♭-9	C-E-G-B♭-D
MAJOR 9th	Cmaj9	1-3-5-7-9	C-E-G-B-D
MINOR 9th	Cm9	1-3♭-5-7♭-9	C-E♭-G-B♭-D
SEVEN FLAT NINE	C7-9	1-3-5-7♭-9♭	C-E-G-B♭-D♭

Chord Spellings

C	C-E-G
Cm	C-Eb-G
Cdim	C-Eb-Gb
C+	C-E-G#
C6	C-E-G-A
Cm6	C-Eb-G-A
C7	C-E-G-Bb
Cmaj7	C-E-G-B
Cm7	C-Eb-G-Bb
Cm7-5	C-Eb-Gb-Bb
Cdim7	C-Eb-Gb-Bbb(A)
C9	C-E-G-B-Bb-D
Cmaj9	C-E-G-B-D
Cm9	C-Eb-G-Bb-D
C7-9	C-E-G-Bb-Db
D	D-F#-A
Dm	D-F-A
Ddim	D-F-Ab
D+	D-F#-A#
D6	D-F#-A-B
Dm6	D-F-A-B
D7	D-F#-A-C
Dmaj7	D-F#-A-C#
Dm7	D-F-A-C
Dm7-5	D-F-Ab-C
Ddim7	D-F-Ab-Cb(B)
D9	D-F#-A-C-E
Dmaj9	D-F#-A-C#-E
Dm9	D-F-A-C-E
D7-9	D-F#-A-C-Eb
F	F-A-C
Fm	F-Ab-C
Fdim	F-Ab-Cb(B)
F+	F-A-C#
F6	F-A-C-D
Fm6	F-Ab-C-D
F7	F-A-C-Eb
Fmaj7	F-A-C-E
Fm7	F-Ab-C-Eb
Fm7-5	F-Ab-Cb(B)-Eb
Fdim7	F-Ab-Cb-Ebb(D)
F9	F-A-C-Eb-G
Fmaj9	F-A-C-E-G
Fm9	F-Ab-C-Eb-G
F7-9	F-A-C-Eb-Gb
G	G-B-D
Gm	G-Bb-D
Gdim	G-Bb-Db
G+	G-B-D#
G6	G-B-D-E
Gm6	G-Bb-D-E
G7	G-B-D-F
Gmaj7	G-B-D-F#
Gm7	G-Bb-D-F
Gm7-5	G-Bb-Db-F
Gdim7	G-Bb-Db-Fb(E)
G9	G-B-D-F-A
Gmaj9	G-B-D-F#-A
Gm9	G-Bb-D-F-A
G7-9	G-B-D-F-Ab
C#	C#-E#(F)-G#
C#m	C#-E-G#
C#dim	C#-E-G
C#+	C#-E#(F)-G##(A)
C#6	C#-E#(F)-G#-A#
C#m6	C#-E-G#-A#
C#7	C#-E#(F)-G#-B
C#maj7	C#-E#(F)-G#-B#(C)
C#m7	C#-E-G#-B
C#m7-5	C#-E-G-B
C#dim7	C#-E-G-Bb
C#9	C#-E#(F)-G#-B-D#
C#maj9	C#-E#(F)-G#-B#(C)-D#
C#m9	C#-E-G#-B-D#
C#7-9	C#-E#(F)-G#-B-D
Eb	Eb-G-Bb
Ebm	Eb-Gb-Bb
Ebdim	Eb-Gb-Bbb(A)
Eb+	Eb-G-B
Eb6	Eb-G-Bb-C
Ebm6	Eb-Gb-Bb-C
Eb7	Eb-G-Bb-Db
Ebmaj7	Eb-G-Bb-D
Ebm7	Eb-Gb-Bb-Db
Ebm7-5	Eb-Gb-Bbb(A)-Db
Ebdim7	Eb-Gb-Bbb(A)-Dbb(C)
Eb9	Eb-G-Bb-Db-F
Ebmaj9	Eb-G-Bb-D-F
Ebm9	Eb-Gb-Bb-Db-F
Eb7-9	Eb-G-Bb-Db-Fb(E)
F#	F#-A#-C#
F#m	F#-A-C#
F#dim	F#-A-C
F#+	F#-A#-C##(D)
F#6	F#-A#-C#-D#
F#m6	F#-A-C#-D#
F#7	F#-A#-C#-E
F#maj7	F#-A#-C#-E#(F)
F#m7	F#-A-C#-E
F#m7-5	F#-A-C-E
F#dim7	F#-A-C-Eb
F#9	F#-A#-C#-E-G#
F#maj9	F#-A#-C#-E#(F)-G#
F#m9	F#-A-C#-E-G#
F#7-9	F#-A#-C#-E-G#
Ab	Ab-C-Eb
Abm	Ab-Cb(B)-Eb
Abdim	Ab-Cb(B)-Ebb(D)
Ab+	Ab-C-E
Ab6	Ab-C-Eb-F
Abm6	Ab-Cb(B)-Eb-F
Ab7	Ab-C-Eb-Gb
Abmaj7	Ab-C-Eb-G
Abm7	Ab-Cb(B)-Eb-Gb
Abm7-5	Ab-Cb(B)-Ebb(D)-Gb
Abdim7	Ab-Cb(B)-Ebb(D)-Gbb(F)
Ab9	Ab-C-Eb-Gb-Bb
Abmaj9	Ab-C-Eb-G-Bb
Abm9	Ab-Cb(B)-Eb-Gb-Bb
Ab7-9	Ab-C-Eb-Gb-Bbb(A)
Db	Db-F-Ab
Dbm	Db-Fb(E)-Ab
Dbdim	Db-Fb(E)-Abb(C)
Db+	Db-F-A
Db6	Db-F-Ab-Bb
Dbm6	Db-Fb(E)-Ab-Bb
Db7	Db-F-Ab-Cb(B)
Dbmaj7	Db-F-Ab-C
Dbm7	Db-Fb(E)-Ab-Cb(B)
Dbm7-5	Db-Fb(E)-Abb(G)-Cb(B)
Dbdim7	Db-Fb(E)-Abb(G)-Cbb(Bb)
Db9	Db-F-Ab-Cb(B)-Eb
Dbmaj9	Db-F-Ab-C-Eb
Dbm9	Db-Fb(E)-Ab-Cb(B)-Eb
Db7-9	Db-F-Ab-Cb(B)-Ebb(D)
E	E-G#-B
Em	E-G-B
Edim	E-G-Bb
E+	E-G#-B#(C)
E6	E-G#-B-C#
Em6	E-G-B-C#
E7	E-G#-B-D
Emaj7	E-G#-B-D#
Em7	E-G-B-D
Em7-5	E-G-Bb-D
Edim7	E-G-Bb-Db
E9	E-G#-B-D-F#
Emaj9	E-G#-B-D#-F#
Em9	E-G-B-D-F#
E7-9	E-G#-B-D-F
Gb	Gb-Bb-Db
Gbm	Gb-Bbb(A)-Db
Gbdim	Gb-Bbb(A)-Dbb(C)
Gb+	Gb-Bb-D
Gb6	Gb-Bb-Db-Eb
Gbm6	Gb-Bbb(A)-Db-Eb
Gb7	Gb-Bb-Db-Fb(E)
Gbmaj7	Gb-Bb-Db-F
Gbm7	Gb-Bbb(A)-Db-Fb(E)
Gbm7-5	Gb-Bbb(A)-Dbb(C)-Fb(E)
Gbdim7	Gb-Bbb(A)-Dbb(C)-Fbb(Eb)
Gb9	Gb-Bb-Db-Fb(E)-Ab
Gbmaj9	Gb-Bb-Db-F-Ab
Gbm9	Gb-Bbb(A)-Db-Fb(E)-Ab
Gb7-9	Gb-Bb-Db-Fb-Abb(G)
A	A-C#-E
Am	A-C-E
Adim	A-C-Eb
A+	A-C#-E#(F)
A6	A-C#-E-F#
Am6	A-C-E-F#
A7	A-C#-E-G
Amaj7	A-C#-E-G#
Am7	A-C-E-G
Am7-5	A-C-Eb-G
Adim7	A-C-Eb-Gb
A9	A-C#-E-G-B
Amaj9	A-C#-E-G#-B
Am9	A-C-E-G-B
A7-9	A-C#-E-G-Bb
Bb	Bb-D-F
Bbm	Bb-Db-F
Bbdim	Bb-Db-Fb(E)
Bb+	Bb-D-F#
Bb6	Bb-D-F-G
Bbm6	Bb-Db-F-G
Bb7	Bb-D-F-Ab
Bbmaj7	Bb-D-F-A
Bbm7	Bb-Db-F-Ab
Bbm7-5	Bb-Db-Fb(E)-Ab
Bbdim7	Bb-Db-Fb(E)-Abb(G)
Bb9	Bb-D-F-Ab-C
Bbmaj9	Bb-D-F-A-C
Bbm9	Bb-Db-F-Ab-C
Bb7-9	Bb-D-F-Ab-Cb(B)
B	B-D#-F#
Bm	B-D-F#
Bdim	B-D-F
B+	B-D#-F##(G)
B6	B-D#-F#-G#
Bm6	B-D-F#-G#
B7	B-D#-F#-A
Bmaj7	B-D#-F#-A#
Bm7	B-D-F#-A
Bm7-5	B-D-F-A
Bdim7	B-D-F-Ab
B9	B-D#-F#-A-C#
Bmaj9	B-D#-F#-A#-C#
Bm9	B-D-F#-A-C#
B7-9	B-D#-F#-A-C

GLOSSARY

A Tempo — return to original tempo.

Accelerando — accelerate (increase) the tempo gradually.

Accent > — play with additional stress, louder.

Accidentals — flat, sharp, and natural signs.

Adagio — slowly, leisurely.

Allegretto — moderately fast.

Allegro — in a lively manner.

Andante — a slow, walking tempo.

Chord — the simultaneous sounding of three of more pitches.

Chord Symbols — letter placed above the staves to indicate the use of particular chords.

CODA ⊕ — ending, concluding passage.

Common Time 𝄴 — meter.

Crescendo (*cresc.*) — gradually louder

Da Capo al Fine (D.C. al Fine) — return to the beginning, play to the Fine marking, the end.

Dal Segno (D.S.) — repeat from the sign.

Decrescendo (*decresc.*) — becoming gradually softer.

Diminuendo (*dim.*) — becoming gradually softer.

Dynamics — relative intensity, loudness.

Enharmonic — pitches that sound the same but have different names.

Fermata ⌒ — a pause in the music; hold the note for extra time.

Fine — the end.

1st & 2nd Endings — symbols indicating to repeat a section of music, playing the first ending the first time and the second ending the second time.

Forte 𝆑 — loud.

Fortissimo 𝆑𝆑 — very loud.

Interval — the distance between two pitches

Key Signature — flats or sharps arranged in a particular order at the beginning of each staff to indicate the key of a composition.

Largo — extremely slow, solemn.

Ledger Lines — short horizontal lines written above or below a clef to extend the staff

Legato — smooth and connected, slurred.

Loco — play notes in normal position as written.

Maestoso — majestically.

Meter — the pattern of regular recurring pulses.

Metronome (M.M.) — a mechanical device that "ticks" the basic pulse at a selected tempo, such as ♩ = 100.

Mezzo forte 𝆐𝆑 — medium loud.

Mezzo piano 𝆐𝆏 — medium quiet.

Moderato — moderate tempo.

Octave Signs 8va — a symbol indicating that pitches are played 1 octave higher, or lower, than written;

15ma — a symbol indicating that pitches are played 2 octaves higher, or lower, than written.

Ostinato — a continually repeated pattern

Phrase — a "sentence" of musical speech.

Pianissimo 𝆏𝆏 — very softly.

Piano 𝆏 — soft.

Poco moto — little motion.

Rallentando — gradually slower.

Repeat :‖ — play the section again.

Risoluto — boldly, decisively.

Ritardando *rit.* — gradually slower.

Scherzo (Scherzando) — fast, playful.

Sforzando 𝆑𝆎 — with a strong accent.

Simile — in a similar manner.

Slur — a curved line above or below a series of notes indicating to play legato.

Staccato — a dot directly above or below a note indicating to play in a detached manner.

Tempo — rate of speed.

Tenuto — sustain for full value.

Tie — connects notes on the same line or space; hold the notes for their combined value.

Triad — three harmonic pitches that sound as a chord, may be major, minor, diminished or augmented.

EXPANSIONS
REPERTOIRE for PIANO

From *Keveren to Kabalevsky,* this series features imaginative original music designed to help developing pianists master the technical and musical concepts needed to play more advanced literature.

Phillip Keveren

The Creation
Early Intermediate Piano Solos
00290438 ....$6.95

Noah's Ark
Late Elementary Piano Solos
00290398 ....$5.95

Tex-Mex Rex & Other Dancing Dinosaurs
Elementary Piano Solos
00290440 ....$5.95

Stephen Covello

Focus On Fun: The Quarter-Note Book
Early Elementary Piano Solos
in Five-Finger Patterns
00290378 ....$5.95

Focus On Fun: The Eighth-Note Book
Elementary Piano Solos
00290416 ....$5.95

Focus On Fun: The Late Elementary Book
Late Elementary Piano Solos
00290419 ....$5.95

Focus On Fun: The Pre-Literature Book
Early Intermediate Piano Solos
00290424 ....$5.95

Bruce Berr

Imaginations In Style
Late Elementary Piano Solos
00290359 ....$5.95

Explorations In Style
Early Intermediate Piano Solos
00290360 ....$5.95

Celebrations In Style
Intermediate Piano Solos
00290361/$6.95

Expeditions In Style
IntermediatePiano Solos
00290433 ....$6.95

Jubilations In Style
Later Intermediate Piano Solos
00290432 ....$6.95

Italo Taranta

Miniature Scenes
Late Elementary Piano Solos
00290356 ....$5.95

Miniature Stories
Early Intermediate Piano Solos
00290357 ....$6.95

Miniature Dramas
Late Intermediate Piano Solos
00290358 ....$6.95

Katherine Glaser

Technique Tunes
Elementary Piano Solos
00290400 ....$6.95

Technique Melodies
Late Elementary Piano Solos
00290399 ....$6.95

Technique Dances
Early Intermediate Piano Solos
00290401 ....$7.95

Bill Boyd

Jazz Starters
Early Elementary Piano Solos
00290425 ....$5.95

Jazz Starters II
Elementary Piano Solos
00290434 ....$5.95

New Composers!

Just Being Me
Elementary Piano Solos
by *Remi Bouchard*
00290439 ....$7.95

School Is Out!
Elementary Piano Solos
by *Barbara Gallagher*
00290421 ,.......................$5.95

Coral Reef Suite
Late Elementary Piano Sol
by *Carol Klose*
00290447 ....$5.

Nature Scenes
Early Intermediate Piano S
by *Kevin Cray*
00290426 ....$5.

Parade To The Circus
Early Intermediate Piano S
by *Susan Sawyer*
00290377 ....$5.

Autumn Sketches
Late Intermediate to Early
Advanced Piano Solos
by *Christos Tsitsaros*
00290418 ....$7

Musings
Early Advanced Piano Sol
by *Francisco Nunez*
00290422 ....$7

Dmitri Kabalevsky

28 Piano Pieces For Children
Early to Late Intermediate
Piano Solos
by *Dmitri Kabalevsky*
00290391 ....$12

FOR MORE INFORMATION, SEE YOUR LOCAL MUSIC DEALER,
OR WRITE TO:

HAL•LEONARD
CORPORATION

7777 W. BLUEMOUND RD. P.O. BOX 13819 MILWAUKEE, WI 53213

Prices, contents, and availability subject to change without notice.
Some products may not be available outside the U.S.A.